Knowledge Management Matters

Words of Wisdom from Leading Practitioners

EDITED BY JOHN & JOANN GIRARD

Published by Sagology, LLLP, Macon, Georgia
www.sagology.com

Please contact info@sagology.com for additional information.

ISBN: 197440319X
ISBN-13: 978-1974403196

CONTENTS

DEDICATION

Dedicated to our next generation of knowledge seekers:
Liz, Cynthia, and Isla

PREFACE

BY JOHN & JOANN GIRARD

Let there be light ...

The catalyst for this book was a desire to help leaders who are interested in knowledge management. To achieve this lofty goal, we reached out to practitioners who we admire in the knowledge management world, to see if they would share what they had learned. We were absolutely delighted with the people who agreed to join the project. Collectively, we know they are most capable of shedding light on a subject that sometimes leaves people in the dark. The result is a book, which is by practitioners and for practitioners.

Knowledge Management Matters: Words of Wisdom from Leading Practitioners is a collection of works penned by this amazing and diverse group of thought leaders. Each of these trailblazers has generously shared their knowledge with a view to helping you and your organization succeed in the knowledge environment. The tips, tactics, and techniques they suggest are time-tested and proven concepts that will help you achieve your organizational objectives. Their collective works are based on decades of experiences with real-world organizations. This is not a book of untested theories that might work, but rather a compilation of genuine *words of wisdom* from experienced KM practitioners who know knowledge management.

Knowledge Management Matters starts with a brief overview of the evolution of knowledge management. Building on this historical foundation, we launch a wide-ranging exploration of the domain. Throughout the book are excellent examples of what works, what doesn't, and some thought-provoking teases about the future. The authors offer great advice on a variety of subjects including storytelling, big data, creativity & innovation, leading communities, knowledge assets, co-creation, catering for a transient workforce and so much more.

A multiplicity of experiences...

As you read the chapters, you will quickly note that there is not unanimity on many of the issues. We very deliberately opted for a group of practitioners who would proffer differing, yet complementary, words of wisdom. Given that consensus on a knowledge management definition has escaped us for decades, it should not be a surprise that there remains multiple interpretations of how best to apply knowledge management. If you are interested in knowledge management definitions, please be sure to visit www.johngirard.net/km where we catalog more than 100 KM definitions.

A quick word on style. We asked the contributors to share their knowledge in the way that worked best for them. Some offered chapters from previously published books, while others opted to write something new. Some felt the first person worked best for their story, while others chose a more formal style. Although we were a little nervous about the rather Laissez-faire style, it turns out, it was a great decision. The diversity of style combined with the variety of experiences proved to be the magic recipe we sought.

Each of the chapters is preceded by a short *About this Chapter* section that sets the scene for the chapter. Reading these passages will be time well spent. Following each chapter is a short *About the Author* section that includes contacts details. We encourage you to reach out to the authors.

We simply cannot thank the remarkable authors enough. They very generously shared their knowledge and for that we owe them a huge debt of gratitude. The practitioners extraordinaire, in alphabetical order, are:

- **Stephanie Barnes**, Director of Doing Things Differently at Art of Innovation
- **Shawn Callahan**, Founder of Anecdote
- **Paul Corney**, Founder of knowledge et al
- **Nancy M. Dixon,** Author of Common Knowledge, HBSP
- **Stan Garfield**, Knowledge Management Author, Speaker, and Community Leader
- **Anthony J. Rhem,** President/Principal Consultant of A.J. Rhem & Associates, Inc.
- **Arthur Shelley**, Founder of Intelligent Answers
- **Douglas Weidner**, Chairman & Chief Instructor of KM Institute
- **Ron Young**, Founder of Knowledge Associates International

We hope you enjoy the book. Be sure to let us know what you think john@johngirard.net or joann@joanngirard.net

SIMPLE IDEAS THAT WORKED IN COMPLEX (2008) ENVIRONMENTS

ABOUT THE CHAPTER

The chapter that follows is a slightly tweaked version of a chapter from our 2009 book, *A leader's guide to knowledge management: Drawing on the past to enhance future performance*, published by Business Expert Press. The purpose of the chapter then, which was originally titled "Simple Ideas That Work in Complex Environments," was to highlight some ideas that we judged as successful knowledge management activities, circa 2008.

The purpose of including the chapter now, in this 2018 book, is to provide a baseline for you to consider the change we have witnessed in a decade. In *The Road Ahead*, Bill Gates wrote "We always overestimate the change that will occur in the next two years and underestimate the change that will occur in the next ten." Gates' quote remains as relevant today as when he penned it more than 20 years ago.

The chapters that follow offer an up-to-date state of knowledge management, as told by nine of the most respected knowledge management practitioners of today. We hope this foundational chapter will provide a historic context to help highlight the great work these folks have done in progressing the domain.

1

SIMPLE IDEAS THAT WORKED IN COMPLEX (2008) ENVIRONMENTS

BY JOHN & JOANN GIRARD

A time-honored consultant's tactic is to ask executives what keeps them awake at night. The answer to this simple question often provides a clue as to the burning platform from which the seasoned consultant may offer advice on how to solve the executive's problems. This does not always work, of course. John once witnessed a very experienced leader answer the question by saying, "My dog, my dog keeps me awake at night." At first, he was taken back. John thought he must be kidding... but he wasn't!

In this chapter, we will review a series of challenges facing the baby-boomer generation of executives and some common solutions with a view to answering the question, Is knowledge power? We will start this exploration by examining why many executives crave the facts. Next, we will consider the rather bizarre concept of unknown unknowns. Along the way, we will explore some time-tested solutions that have helped baby-boomer executives create knowledge-empowered organizations. To navigate the many success stories—and some not so successful stories—we will use Nonaka's infamous SECI (socialization, externalization, combination, and internationalization) model as a map.

Just the Facts, Please

Let's face it, executives are busy people, and they do not have time for extra words, especially pronouns. How many times have you heard an executive say, "I just want the facts"? But do you as an executive really want the facts? Remember that in a previous chapter data was defined as a set of discrete, objective facts about events. We suggest that from a management perspective two features are worthy of note. The first of these was data is the lowest level in the value chain and by itself is not very beneficial. Arguably, too much data exists and until or unless managers transform this data into information, it is simply occupying valuable space.

So why is it that executives crave data? If they buy into the concepts of knowledge management, then one would think that they should prefer having access to processed data, which many people call information or maybe even knowledge. Recall Peter Drucker's description, "Information is data endowed with relevance and purpose" (1988, p. 46), which seems to imply that senior managers would wish for this relevant entity (information) rather than the raw form (data). However, no matter how many times they remind themselves of this concept, the executives continue to say, "I want the facts." Well, maybe the answer is to give them facts, but in a way that can make a difference.

Previously, we suggested that combination was the preferred way for Westerners or Occidentals to create knowledge. Some would suggest that such a statement is a hasty generalization, and we admit that could be true. However, before admitting defeat we would like to know how many times have you heard an executive say, "Can you run the numbers on that?" or "What happens if you combine that data with last quarter's data?" or many similar questions. The reality is, we would argue, that many of us like to create new knowledge by combining two or more sources of explicit data. We will use this idea of combination to begin our examination of knowledge management in action.

In the first chapter of our book *A Leader's Guide to Knowledge Management*, we critiqued the Tofflers for using a broad definition of knowledge. We argued that it is important to be able to differentiate between the three terms and then we went on, at great length, to describe the difference between the three terms. Although we believe it is important to understand the difference, especially from an academic point of view, we know that when a tough decision must be made the last thing an executive is considering is the difference between three related concepts. What executives need, and need now, is whatever nugget will help them make a decision.

One of the real problems with the pyramid concept of data, information, and knowledge is that the boundaries are not clear. What is data to one person may be knowledge to another. At the end of the day, executives crave whatever is needed to make a decision; they do not worry about the nomenclature. Verna Allee, author of several excellent knowledge management books, reminds us that "fuzzy boundaries create innovation" (Allee, 2003, p. 4). This phase was the catalyst for a new model to describe the relationship between data management, information management, and knowledge management. Rather than focus on whether a particular tool, tactic, or technique should be labeled as a data management, information management, or knowledge management, the model suggests that a continuum exists. By eliminating strict boundaries, which are often difficult to define, the model focuses on outputs rather than preconceived categorizations.

Creating Knowledge With Data

Data mining is an excellent example of this concept in action. Some would argue that data mining is data-dependent and therefore a data management tool. Others argue that data mining was not possible until powerful information technology systems were available to take deep dives into the vast stores of data and therefore it must be an information management tool. Still others contend that data mining is clearly knowledge management. At the end of the day, the executive who makes a vital decision because of a particular process is more concerned with the result than the label.

Consider the following example of data mining in action. According to NCR Corporation, one of its divisions (Teradata)

> pioneered the field of data mining by looking at sales data from a retailer and discovering that in the evening hours, beer and diapers are often purchased together. This relationship, called a data mining affinity, captured the imagination of industry watchers, spawning a legend that has been recounted hundreds of times and is frequently cited as the textbook example of data mining. (Michael, 2002)

Much has been written about this example of data mining in action. Many of the articles describe the technology used to discover this relationship while others describe the mathematics used to develop the algorithms.

However, the aspect of most interest to us is what the retailer did with this valuable information. Imagine that you are at the helm of a large retail operation and you are presented with the findings of this experimental research. At an executive meeting, the vice president of sales, supported by the chief information officer, describe their findings. They tell a story that every Friday evening, most people who purchase beer also purchase diapers. They have the data to prove it; each and every Friday there is a very clear relationship between beer sales and diapers sales.

The question is, what do you do armed with this *knowledge?* Most executives would consider how they could use this *knowledge* to create a competitive advantage. They would realize the value of this *knowledge* is time limited. In other words, once their competitors discover the relationship, the value of the *knowledge* will be diminished. Before answering the question, how many executives would stop to ask the question, Am I dealing with data, information, or knowledge? None. Well, no executive who wants to remain competitive would pause to answer such a trivial question. The reality is, executives are not concerned with the nomenclature, but rather with the results.

So what really happened? What did the retailer do? This is where the urban myth part of the story starts. Many tales have been told about the unnamed retailer—so many that many skeptics suggest the whole event may not have existed. Like many great stories, the most important thing is the story must be believable; it does not have to be true, but it does have to be believable. But more about stories later.

When John shares this story of data mining in action with his Master's level knowledge management students, he asks the students what they think happened. Predictably, there is a group of students that suggest that beer and diapers would be put together in some convenient location, perhaps near the front of the store. A second group usually emerges arguing that the beer should be put at one end of the store with the diapers at the far end. Some continue by suggesting that we could strategically locate other convenience items along the route. Each of these courses of action seems reasonable.

Many of the students are surprised when John suggests the CEO decided to do nothing. He continues by saying that the CEO was very impressed with the discovery and that she complimented the VP Sales and CIO. After describing how valuable this knowledge was, the CEO announces that the company will not make any changes because of the revelation. The CEO continues by saying that she believes that encouraging the purchase of beer and diapers was not something she wished to pursue. She finishes her discourse by saying, "Knowledge is power—having the supporting data to make this decision was extremely valuable."

The most important point in this story is that the CEO had the data, information, or knowledge (whatever you wish to call it) that she needed to make the decision. We can debate the decision, but at the end of the day, the most important issue is that the CEO had what she needed to make an important corporate decision. Knowledge management is about making sure that senior executives know what they need to know to make the decisions that they must make.

Some people question the authenticity of the beer and diapers story. In fact, many of John's students ask for other examples of data mining in action. One of the challenges with the beer and diapers example is that it took place in 1991. Correctly, graduate students are very skeptical of events that were pioneered when they were in grade school and are still being highlighted as the way of the future. In fact, we encourage this skepticism of ideas that remain immature after a decade and half.

Although many people, students and executives alike, appreciate how data mining could be used to create a competitive advantage, they seek real examples of the technique that have demonstrated and measurable results. Anticipating this question, John goes to class prepared to tell another compelling story about data mining.

The lead in to the story goes something like this. What do you think the Wal-Mart corporation rushes to its own stores in areas where a hurricane is predicted? The usual answers are flashlights, water, batteries, and the like. Most students are surprised to hear that Wal-Mart ships strawberry-flavored Kellogg's Pop-Tarts to areas threatened by hurricanes. The follow-on question is usually, Why would they ship Pop-Tarts? The answer is very simple; Wal-Mart regularly mines the trillions of bytes of data they collect from consumers looking for relationships. Perhaps more astonishing is what they find. For example, Wal-Mart discovers a sevenfold sales increase of Pop-Tarts ahead of hurricanes (Hays, 2004).

Some students will dig a little deeper and demand to know why. Why is it that consumers like to purchase Pop-Tarts ahead of a storm? The short answer is no one is quite sure. There are likely marketing students across the country trying to answer this exact question. They are busy creating consumer surveys that will be used to collect data that will be analyzed, and with a bit of luck they will be able to explain this heretofore-unpredictable consumer activity. In two or three years, we will know the answer to this question.

But wait, can we compete with Wal-Mart or other data miners if we study the problem for 2 years and then we are in a position to explain why consumers did something 2 years ago? Of course not. Wal-Mart calls their data-mining effort *predictive technology;* others are calling it a *data-driven weapon* illustrating the warlike atmosphere of retailing today. By the time others explain why people bought Pop-Tarts during Hurricane Frances, Wal-Mart will be predicting, very accurately, what consumers will purchase during the next disaster (Hays, 2004).

Before leaving the Wal-Mart example, there is one more issue that should be addressed. We are often asked what else sells well ahead of a hurricane. According to Wal-Mart, another pre-hurricane top seller is, well you guessed it, beer. Therefore, a cunning retailer might assume that diapers should also sell well!

Combination—It's Not Always Good!

The two stories of data mining in action are excellent examples of what Nonaka termed combination in the SECI model. By combining two or more pieces of explicit data, we have created new knowledge. In these cases, the knowledge appears to have created a competitive advantage, which of course is a good thing. You may recall that earlier we were quite critical of Westerners' use of combination as a knowledge-creation technique and now we are promoting it as a way to create a competitive advantage.

As is often the case, there are good and bad examples of many tools and techniques. The basis of our criticism is that many Westerners believe that simply combining two pieces of explicit knowledge will ensure new knowledge is created. Let us share a couple of examples of combination not really adding value—both of which are very close to home!

At a 2004 knowledge management conference, the keynote speaker suggested that little new or interesting had been published in the knowledge management domain for some time. The speaker, an author himself, lamented about the repetition that is commonplace in many recent books. He argued that the study of knowledge management has not advanced much since the seminal works of Nonaka and Takeuchi (*The Knowledge-Creating Company*), Davenport and Prusak (*Working Knowledge*), and perhaps a couple others. His underlying point was that authors were not creating new knowledge but rather just repackaging the same old knowledge. In other words, the combination of explicit knowledge did not necessarily create new knowledge. Ironically, he was at the conference to launch a new knowledge management book!

In the early 2000s, our son, John, was serving aboard a Canadian warship in the Persian Gulf, as part of Operation *Enduring Freedom*. His ship was part of a larger formation known as the USS *George Washington* battlegroup, aptly named because the lead ship in the group was the aircraft carrier USS *George Washington*. All total, there were six ships in this futuristic flotilla, each of which were in constant contact with the mother ship. Gone are the days where ships pass in the night without notice. Gone are the days when ships rely on semaphore or even radios to stay in contact. In fact, today's modern warships are one of the best examples of virtual collaboration in action. Each ship is inextricably connected to the remainder of the flotilla.

At the personal level, technology played an important role in ensuring our son was able to stay connected with his friends and family back home. In modern navies, this homeward-bound connection may be as important as the interconnectedness of the operational ships. Though it may be true that Napoleon's armies could "march on food," soldiers, sailors, and airmen and women today are probably more concerned about staying connected than they are about the quality or quantity of their food. If you are in doubt, simply ask a soldier if he or she would rather have a MRE (meal ready to eat, which is actually an oxymoron) or a 5-minute phone call home.

One day, during his 6-month "cruise" in the Persian Gulf, our son decided to explore other opportunities in the military. Although we are not entirely certain what triggered this sudden quest for knowledge, we were very impressed that modern satellite technology allowed him to search the vast stores of data on the Defence Wide Area Network. He was able to access, almost instantly, all the information he wanted to decide what military occupation would be of most interest to him. He was able to read fact sheets and download and watch videos that described each job. Essentially, he had access to everything that would have been available to him if he was back home—very impressive.

He also had access to vast volumes of regulations that explain the process for changing careers. As you can imagine, it is a very bureaucratic process to change careers in the military. There are many forms to fill out and many deadlines to meet. As he continued to navigate through this maze of *knowledge*, he began to trip on contradictions. He found different dates, different processes, and different approval authorities. The more he searched, the more contradictions he found. Soon it became clear that he would not be able to rely on the data he was finding—it was simply impossible to determine which documents were up-to-date and which ones were dangerous old relics taking up valuable space.

At the end of the day, our son contacted us for help. He knew that we would know someone who would have the *real* knowledge he needed. Indeed, he was correct, and after just a couple of telephone calls, we were able to connect with the person who knew the real procedures. This is a great example of how knowledge flows in many organizations. Frequently it makes more sense to find a person who knows what you need to know rather than search volumes of uncontrolled content on corporate intranets.

This story illustrates several crucial points. First, organizations should have procedures for content management and digital asset management; in short, someone should own all data and be responsible to maintain it. However, technology alone will not suffice. Often people prefer to connect with other people rather than the data. To satisfy this want, organizations should consider investing in systems to facilitate this human-to-human connection such as *yellow pages* or *expert location systems*, both of which will be explored in more detail later in the book.

Stories of Simple Ideas That Work in Complex Environments

For several years, we have had the great pleasure of speaking to groups of organizational leaders about knowledge management. Specifically, we speak about how leaders may reap the benefits of creating and sharing organizational knowledge. This journey has taken us to destinations across the United States and Canada as well as Europe, Asia, South America, Africa, and Australia. In fact, Antarctica is the only continent where we have not spoken about knowledge management—we await an invitation!

Over the years, our talks have changed. Initially, we spoke about rather complex cognitive theories with the hope that folks in the audience would take our *words of wisdom* and single-handedly transform their organizations. After many sessions of watching yet another audience grin politely as we delivered our sermon, we realized that we were contributing to one of the common themes of our talks—*information overload.*

As it turns out, much of what we were talking about was simply *lost in the translation.* At first, we wondered if it was the audiences because it certainly could not be us! After each presentation, we would spend hours answering e-mails from individuals with questions such as "I really enjoyed your talk; however, I am not really sure how to implement the ideas you were discussing. Do you have any examples of these ideas in action?" After many nights of responding to similar questions, we realized (finally) that we were making the whole thing seem very complicated.

We began to respond to questions with short stories that illustrated the point we were trying to make. Most of these stories were based on real organizations—although we would often change the names to protect the innocent, like Joe Friday from Dragnet. One day we had an epiphany: Why wait until after the presentation to share these stories? We decided to transform our talks into a series of stories that explained the (unnecessarily) complicated theories we were describing. The rest, as they say, is history.

This was the genesis of a presentation titled *Simple Ideas That Work in Complex Environments*. The premise was rather simple (pun intended): to describe some ideas, many of which were grounded in complicated cognitive theories, that seemed to work in complex environments. What, you may ask, is a complex environment? We opted to use Merriam-Webster's definition for complex: "a group of obviously related units of which the degree and nature of the relationship is imperfectly known" ("complex," 2009). This terse definition describes so many of the organizations in which we have worked, studied, or consulted. The final clause seemed to be key: "the degree and nature of the relationship is imperfectly known."

The data-mining stories in the previous section, as well as the stories that follow, are from the collection of the stories that we use in our talks. The anthology includes original stories, classic stories, stories based on television commercials, stories that have helped guide great organizations, and stories from exceptional leaders (such as the one below). Although the origin of each story is very different, we believe that they all share the common theme of simplifying complex environments. Of course, you are the real judge; let us know what you think. Many of the stories have transcended the boundaries of our talks—we now use them in a variety of venues including graduate and undergraduate management classes, corporate training events, and consulting. Three of our favorites are below.

Unknown Unknowns—Gibberish or Wisdom?

The Plain English Campaign is a United Kingdom–based organization that describes itself as "an independent pressure group fighting for public information to be written in plain English" ("Plain English Campaign," 2006). Annually, the Plain English Campaign presents a variety of awards focusing on the use of English. One of their awards is titled the *Foot in Mouth*, which they present to a public figure for a baffling quote. In 2003, the recipient of the *Foot in Mouth* award was former U.S. Defense Secretary

Donald Rumsfeld for saying the following during a Pentagon press conference on February 12, 2002:

> As we know, there are known knowns; there are things we know we know. We also know there are known unknowns; that is to say we know there are some things we do not know. But there are also unknown unknowns—the ones we don't know we don't know. And if one looks throughout the history of our country and other free countries, it is the latter category that tend to be the difficult ones. ("DoD News Briefing—Secretary Rumsfeld and Gen. Myers," 2002)

Say what? What do you mean there are known knowns, known unknowns, and unknown unknowns? This sounds like gibberish at best or perhaps just pure nonsense. Many journalist poked fun at Donald Rumsfeld, and a series of Internet sites emerged to document the *poetry* of Rumsfeld. Surely, the Secretary misspoke or was misquoted. In fact, nothing could be further from the truth as Donald Rumsfeld very concisely described a major complex management challenge. The challenge is best illustrated using a 2 x 2 matrix:

Unknown Knowns	Unknown Unknowns
Known Knowns	Known Unknonws

Figure 1-1. Rumsfeld's Unknown Unknowns

The point that Secretary Rumsfeld so eloquently articulated in just 20 seconds has since been the subject of a variety of articles and book chapters. Take for example Alex and David Bennet's chapter titled "Exploring the Unknown" in their book *Organizational Survival in the New World: The Intelligent Complex Adaptive System*. This chapter focuses on "how do we identify things that we don't know we don't know" (Bennet & Bennet, 2004). This is exactly what Rumsfeld was suggesting. If we know that we do not know something, then we can develop a plan to find out more. Likewise, if we do not know that we know something, then again we can develop a plan to find the missing link.

Both of these issues are dealt with during external and internal scanning, competitive intelligence, and the like.

The 2 x 2 matrix is a useful way to categorize the challenges confronting many originations. Unfortunately, most leaders focus on the easy bits: things they know and things that they know that they do not know. Many organizations ignore the upper right-hand quadrant—the unknown unknowns—because it is just too difficult. Perhaps some ignore this quadrant because they do not know what to do. A very good example of a time-tested tool to conquer this quadrant is data mining, as we discussed earlier in this chapter. That said, to some degree, the avoidance of the upper right-hand quadrant is a symptom of the *not on my watch syndrome*. Many leaders do not wish to dig too deep into the unknown unknowns because it is uncharted territory. Equally concerning is the fear that discovering unknown unknowns will expose a corporate Achilles heel. Then what would we do?

The other quadrant that often creates anxiety is the upper left or unknown knowns quadrant. One of our favorite stories about this quadrant features a large technology company. The story is loosely based on a real company, but given we embellished a few parts to make our point, we must declare it is a fictional company—let us call them IQ. IQ is a well-known brand that for many years operated with a divisional organization structure. Once a year, each of the divisional vice presidents were afforded the opportunity to brief the Board of Directors on their plans for the future. This rare occasion was seen to be a time when senior executives could describe the next big thing that would provide IQ with a competitive advantage.

One year, the printer division's vice president was extremely excited about his time with the Board. He was sure the directors would agree that his new idea, a printer that could also scan, would be a history-making innovative product, a must-have for many small businesses. The R&D arm of the printer division had been working secretly on the project for some time. After investing considerable resources, their prototype was ready to be showcased to the Board. They were very proud of their clandestine operation; it was quite a coup that none of the technology press had picked up on their work.

Finally, the big day arrived. The vice president was waiting patiently in the anteroom reviewing his presentation. Suddenly, an unprecedented level of applause from inside the boardroom interrupted his thoughts. Shortly afterward the vice president of the scanner division emerged, smiling, and clearly happy with her performance in the room. The printer executive politely asked his colleague why the Board erupted into applause. After a short pause, she replied, "I just showed the Board our prototype for the next big thing… a scanner that can also print." Needless to say, the printer executive was no longer excited about briefing the Board.

The moral of the story is that a *need to know* culture, which is commonplace in many technology companies, does not facilitate knowledge sharing. Here is a case where senior executives did not share, let alone collaborate on the project. Imagine if the two divisions shared resources and knowledge to design the printer scanner. Regrettably, many organizations fall victim to the unknown knowns because they do not foster a collaborative environment with a need to share philosophy.

We Have a Problem!

The nightmare scenario for many executives is a call in the night that begins with the words, "We have a problem!" Almost certainly one of the most famous problems was in April 1970 when astronaut Jack Swigert, aboard *Apollo 13*, radioed Houston and said the famous, but oft misquoted, phrase "Houston, we've had a problem!" Fortunately, most management decisions are not life and death as was the case with *Apollo 13*.

Nevertheless, organizations must be prepared for crisis decision making. It is too late to consider what values are important to an organization when crises present themselves. The recent and spectacular failures of large corporations seem to indicate that many corporate leaders are ill prepared or unwilling to deal with unanticipated tribulations. However, there are a few great examples of organizations whose management teams internalize core values in quiet times so that they are prepared for catastrophic events.

In 1943, when General Robert Wood Johnson penned "Our Credo" for Johnson & Johnson, he had no idea just how important this short passage would become. He had no idea how his carefully crafted words would help the leaders of the next generation. The Credo has been changed, ever so slightly, since 1943; however, most of the changes have been in language and not in substance or spirit. The Credo begins by stating, "We believe our first responsibility is to the doctors, nurses and patients, to mothers and fathers and all others who use our products and services. In meeting their needs everything we do must be of high quality." The Credo continues with some guiding principles and then concludes by stating, "When we operate according to these principles, the stockholders should realize a fair return" (see http://tinyurl.com/c7rtfa for the complete text of the one-page Credo).

The Credo proved its worth when some malefactors infected some Tylenol with cyanide in 1982. According to Lawrence G. Foster, vice president of public relations for Johnson & Johnson, "The Credo served the company better than any crisis management plan could have" (Foster, 1983). Based on the Credo, the Johnson & Johnson managers knew what to do. However, how can a 40-year-old one-page document help managers make decisions? The answer is that everyone in Johnson & Johnson is aware of the Credo and its importance. It is more than words on a paper. It is more than just some poster hanging in conference rooms. It has become synonymous with Johnson & Johnson, and all managers know what it means.

All too often, executives go through the motions of developing a mission, vision, and values so that they may be proudly displayed in offices. To many, this is a paper exercise that does not really change the price of fish. Johnson & Johnson's Credo is NOT simply a paper exercise. Johnson & Johnson's Credo is a guiding document that has passed the test of time, and it is an excellent example of what Nonaka termed internalization.

A Day to Remember

For many of us, August 14, 2003, is a date we will remember. That was the day that some 50 million Americans and Canadians witnessed a blackout across the Northeast portion of the North American continent. On that hot August day, we were living in Ottawa, Canada's capital. Brownouts, a temporary reduction in electric power, are relatively common in Ontario during the summer and although local blackouts are not unheard of, they are quite rare. The "usual suspect" in these cases is high summer temperatures, which in turn cause people to crank up their air conditioners. Invariably this puts a strain on the power grid and sometimes the result is a brownout or very occasionally a blackout.

We knew this day was different when we received a telephone call from our daughter, Terri-Lynn. At the time, she was a Human Resource Associate at Wal-Mart in Ottawa. We were not surprised when she told us that her store was using emergency power as our house was without electricity and it was only about 2 miles from her office. What really surprised us was when she said that she had just spoken to a Toronto store and it, too, was experiencing a blackout. Her colleague stated that the entire metropolitan Toronto area was in the dark. All of a sudden, the situation changed. How could Ottawa (population 800,000) and Toronto (population 2,500,000) be without electricity?

We turned on a battery-powered radio to discover that New York and Detroit were also without power. If the news reports were true, then at least 15 million people were in the dark, maybe even more. How could this be? Not surprisingly, there was talk of malicious attacks. This seemed plausible. Now what?

Well, in hindsight we now know that this was not caused by a targeted attacked on the North American infrastructure but rather an unfortunate, though predictable, shutdown designed to protect the grid. The real question becomes, What should we do to ensure this never happens again? One way is to conduct an After Action Review, or AAR, which considers four questions:

1. What was supposed to happen?
2. What happened?
3. What is the difference?

4. What should we do to improve?

The U.S. Army designed the AAR process more than two decades ago. The premise is simple—how can we learn from our mistakes to ensure we do not repeat the same mistakes? We like to think about it as a scheme that encourages making "new" mistakes rather than the same old ones. Of course, for the U.S. Army it is much more serious than avoiding old mistakes because an avoidable mistake may be dire—it may involve the loss of life of a brave American soldier and we must avoid that at all costs.

Today many organizations are benefiting from the outstanding work of the U.S. Army; organizations across the United States and around the world have implemented AARs to ensure they make new mistakes. AARs are a powerful concept for creating and transferring organizational knowledge; however, like many management processes, they must be implemented with care.

Often it is a good idea to have a trained facilitator help organizations learn the craft of AARs. Once AARs become commonplace, they should be conducted by internal managers. Remember, AARs are not about assigning or implying blame, but rather, AARs are about making sure that organizations do not repeat the same mistakes. AAR sessions should be short and positive. Do NOT allow the sessions to turn into a witch hunt or a finger-pointing exercise. AARs are a very good example of what Nonaka termed Externalization. By the way, it turns out the cause of the blackout of 2003 was likely due to trees not being trimmed as they should have been.

Remember Donald Rumsfeld

The poetry of former Secretary Donald Rumsfeld is frequently mocked. Regrettably, the mockers of his words of wisdom often miss the point and the real lessons are lost in the laughter. Rumsfeld's unknown unknowns speech is one that should not be mocked, ignored, or forgotten. Some executives will recognize the brilliance of his words; the most successful executives will heed his advice and dedicate resources to learning about unknown unknowns. Data mining is a useful tool in this quest.

Now You Know...

- Executives frequently crave the *facts*; however, it is often better to provide knowledge that will support decision making.
- Data mining is a powerful technique for discovering rather bizarre but very useful data anomalies.
- Leaders should ensure that the content on organizational intranets, portals, and the like is not out of date.
- Thinking about unknown unknowns may well reap benefits.

- Johnson & Johnson's Credo provides an excellent example of knowledge internalization in action.
- An After Action Review, or AAR, is a post-event knowledge capture process that considers four questions:
  1. What was supposed to happen?
  2. What happened?
  3. What is the difference?
  4. What should we do to improve?

ABOUT THE AUTHORS

John P. Girard, Ph.D. holds the Peyton Anderson Endowed Chair in Information Technology at Middle Georgia State University's School of Information Technology. He is a professor, storyteller, and adventurer who has enjoyed the privilege of speaking to leaders on six continents about technology, leadership, and culture. Engaging with students daily ensures he remains current in the ever-changing world in which we live and do business. John has traveled to 116 countries investigating globalization and innovation in action. Prior to transitioning to the academy, John was acting Director of Knowledge Management at National Defence Headquarters in Ottawa, Canada. He served for 24 years in the Canadian Forces, retiring at the rank of Lieutenant-Colonel. To learn more about John, visit www.johngirard.net

JoAnn Girard is the co-founder and managing partner of Sagology, a firm that focuses on connecting people with people to collaborate and share knowledge. She has worked on a variety of knowledge intensive research projects, which considered issues such as information anxiety, enterprise dementia, and organizational memories. Prior to forming Sagology, JoAnn was co-founder of two successful technology companies. Before entering the high-tech arena JoAnn worked in the travel industry and as a school librarian. The experience she gained in these information intensive positions proved especially valuable as she considers the knowledge challenges confronting executives today.

JoAnn and John have published five books together: A Leader's Guide to Knowledge Management: Drawing on the Past to Enhance Future Performance (Business Expert Press, 2009), Social Knowledge: Using Social Media to Know What You Know (IGI Global, 2011), Business Goes Virtual: Realizing the Value of Collaboration, Social and Virtual Strategies (Business Expert Press, 2011) and Tips for Two: Tales of a Globetrotting Couple (Sagology, 2013) and Sage Sayings: Inspiring Native American Passages for Leaders (Sagology, 2014).

BIBLIOGRAPHY

Allee, V. (2003). *The future of knowledge: Increasing prosperity through value networks*. Amsterdam; Boston: Butterworth-Heinemann.

Bennet, A., & Bennet, D. (2004). *Organizational survival in the new world: The intelligent complex adaptive system*. Amsterdam; Boston: Butterworth-Heinemann.

Complex. (2009). In Merriam-Webster online dictionary. Retrieved March 11, 2009, from http://www.merriam-webster.com/dictionary/complex

Davenport, T. H., & Prusak, L. (1998). *Working knowledge: How organizations manage what they know*. Boston: Harvard Business School Press.

DoD News Briefing—Secretary Rumsfeld and Gen. Myers. (2002, February 12). Retrieved July 6, 2006, from http://www.defenselink.mil/transcripts/2002/t02122002_t212sdv2.html

Drucker, P. F. (1988). The coming of the new organization. *Harvard Business Review, 66*(1), 45.

Foster, L. G. (1983). The Johnson & Johnson credo and the Tylenol crisis. *New Jersey Bell Journal, 6*(1), 6.

Gates, B., Myhrvold, N., & Rinearson, P. (1996). *The road ahead* (Completely rev. and up-to-date. ed.). New York: Penguin Books.

Hays, C. L. (2004, November 14). What Wal-Mart knows about customers' habits. *New York Times*.

Michael, H. (2002). *Teradata takes data mining beyond beer and diapers*. Dayton, OH: NCR Corporation.

Nonaka, I., & Takeuchi, H. (1995). *The knowledge-creating company: How Japanese companies create the dynamics of innovation*. New York: Oxford University Press.

Plain English Campaign. Retrieved July 6, 2006, from http://www.plainenglish .co.uk

Toffler, A., & Toffler, H. (1993). *War and anti-war: Survival at the dawn of the 21st century* (1st ed.). Boston: Little, Brown.

THE THREE ERAS OF KNOWLEDGE MANAGEMENT

ABOUT THE CHAPTER

In the late 1990s, I was at an early KM conference when an editor from the Harvard Business School Press said that HBSP was interested in this thing they had heard about called knowledge management. I was then a professor at the George Washington University (GW), and the editor knew I researched and had written a book about Organizational Learning, a close cousin to knowledge management. She asked me if I wanted to write a book that explained what knowledge management was. Wow, who wouldn't want to write for HBSP!!! I said YES.

I decided to interview companies, anywhere in the world, that had a reputation for really making KM work. I figured that way I would discover what they had in common and could write the book on how to do KM. E&Y gave me a little travel money and off I went to interview at fifteen companies, Ford, BP, TI, and the US Army among them. I saw a lot of different KM processes. Everybody appeared to be doing something different, and everybody was succeeding. That was not what I had hoped to find; I was looking for the one right answer! But when I sat down and began to analyze all the data I had collected, I realized three factors influenced the type of KM process that different organizations were using. One was the nature of the task, that is, was this task something that was done over and over again the same way, like building cars at a Ford factory or was the task different every time it was done, like the exploration for oil at BP. A second factor was whether the knowledge that was being transferred to others was explicit or tacit - can it be written down or does it require a conversation to transfer it. And third, how similar or different was the context of the receiver of the knowledge from the context of the group that originated it – how much did the receiver have to change what the other had learned to make it work in their context. Using those factors, I built a framework to guide users in choosing the knowledge transfer processes for their setting. I had my book!

The book, Common Knowledge, took off. I fell in love with KM and left GW to do hands-on KM work with companies. Over the last 17 years, I have continued working and learning about KM as it has developed and matured. What I am writing about in this chapter is how KM has changed during that 17-year journey and what has changed about making it work.

This chapter is:

Please cite as:

Dixon, N.M. (2018). The three eras of knowledge management. In J. P. Girard & J. L. Girard (Eds.), *Knowledge management matters: Words of wisdom from leading practitioners* (19-47). Macon, GA: Sagology

2

THE THREE ERAS OF KNOWLEDGE MANAGEMENT

BY NANCY M. DIXON

KM has changed in many ways since its beginning now almost twenty years ago, with many new tools and strategies. But what is most interesting to me is the profound change in the way we conceptualize knowledge and the implications of that conceptualization for how we do our work as knowledge professionals. What I mean when I say, "how we conceptualize knowledge" are issues like, "Who in the organization has useful knowledge;" "How stable is knowledge over time;" "How we can tell if knowledge is valid or trustworthy." These are not trivial issues because how we conceptualize knowledge greatly impacts the way we design our KM systems and strategies.

If the goal of KM is, as I believe it to be, to leverage the collective knowledge in an organization – then we have been learning how to do KM since early in the 90's. It has been a steep learning curve and we probably still have a steep curve ahead of us, but we are learning as evidenced by how our thinking about dealing with knowledge has changed and evolved.

I organize this evolving landscape into three categories that I think of as eras because each is quite different regarding how knowledge is conceptualized. The first is <u>leveraging explicit knowledge</u> and it is about capturing documented knowledge and creating a collection from it - connecting people to content. The second category is about <u>leveraging experiential knowledge,</u> and it gave rise to communities of practice and social networks. It is primarily a focus on connecting people to people. The third category is about <u>leveraging collective knowledge,</u> and it is primarily about creating new knowledge and innovation, both through online tools like crowdsourcing and through face-to-face conversations like those embedded in Agile and Working Out Loud. It is about connecting ideas to other ideas.

For each category I will describe, 1) how those who were leading the field of KM conceptualized knowledge, 2) the strategies those concepts engendered, and 3) the difficulties and successes those strategies and conceptualizations presented to the field of KM.

Before I describe the three eras in detail, let's back up to what was happening before the advent of knowledge management. Then, if organizations thought about knowledge at all, they thought of it as the content of training classes, and that training was focused on individual development. For example, in the 1980's there was a great interest in competency models, many of which were further developed into instruments to determine what training was needed for an employee in a specific job, or if an employee was qualified for a new job. The underlying assumption of that pre-KM period was that if the organization trained each individual with the competencies required for their specific job, the combined effort would lead to organizational effectiveness - a kind of additive view of organizational knowledge. I was a part of that period and remember how hard we struggled to word competencies, so they could be actionable and measurable.

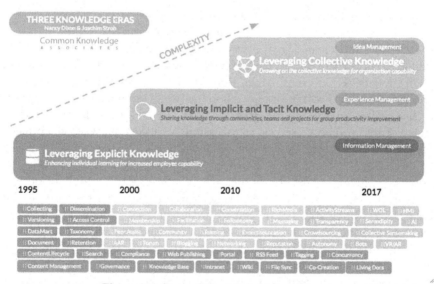

Figure 2-1. Eras of Knowledge Management

Following on the heels of the competency push, was Organizational Learning or the Learning Organization, depending on what you were reading at the time. Senge's book, The Fifth Discipline, came out in 1990 and my book, the Organizational Learning Cycle, was published in 1994. The focus was on how learning could be used to change organizations especially by improving team learning. There were also a number of whole system change efforts, where the whole organization or representatives from the whole organization gathered to solve organizational problems or develop strategy. Those whole system change efforts included Future Search, Open Space Technology, Action Learning, and GE's Workout, among others.

The diagram shows the three eras with a beginning date, but each era continues past where the next era begins. I have extended each category for three reasons, one, many of the strategies prominent in each category have continued to remain viable, two, over time new strategies have been developed to address the basic idea of that category and three, as new organizations take up KM their initial entry tends to be focused on the earlier categories.

Leveraging Explicit Knowledge - ERA 1

Philosophically the beginnings of knowledge management drew most directly from Peter Drucker, who wrote about the Knowledge Age. In his book, The Post-Capitalistic Society (Drucker,1994) predicted the knowledge-based economy, noting that wealth and power, which had previously been based on property and capital, was shifting and would increasingly be based on knowledge. He coined the term "knowledge worker," to describe a new kind of worker doing a new kind of work in the knowledge age.

Building on Drucker's framing, the new way of thinking about knowledge that began in the mid-90s (the lower bar on my diagram) was that knowledge was an organizational asset and if an asset, then it needed to be managed. After all, organizations manage their other assets, e.g., capital, property, people, so it made sense to also manage an organization's knowledge – thus the term (which nearly everyone now regrets) "knowledge management." CEOs began to declare, "Knowledge is our competitive advantage."

The early thinking about how organizations should manage this knowledge asset, was to use technology, taking advantage of the new and growing capability of intranets. There was an effort to collect all the important knowledge that an organization possessed into one database. The analogy was a warehouse or a library. An organization's knowledge would be placed in the warehouse and those that needed it could take the knowledge out and use it. Knowledge was thought of as stable, much like the contents of real warehouses. That is, you could put knowledge in the warehouse today and get it out in six months or even two years later, without any degradation of its value. In this first era of knowledge management, knowledge repositories were the strategy of choice, and they contained best practices and lessons learned as well as a great many technical documents which had previously resided in spiral notebooks.

Management was greatly concerned about the quality and validity of the knowledge being captured. The salient question was, how can we be certain that a practice is "best." To address this issue, many organizations brought together teams of experts from each field of expertise to identify and then write up the best practices for that field. In other organizations, everyone was invited to contribute, then a panel of experts would vet the contributions so that only the "best" made it into the repository. At Chevron, experts categorized employee contributions into levels, e.g., "local practice," "good practice," "validated practice," all the way to "best practice." Having identified the "best practice" some organizations required everyone to implement those practices, making knowledge management a move toward standardization. The assumption was that there was one best way to accomplish any task – so knowledge management professionals were expected to identify and then capture that best way.

Repositories became so ubiquitous that in many organizations the term "knowledge repository" was synonymous with "knowledge management." And since IT (Information Technology) necessarily built or bought the software for the repositories, KM was frequently housed within the IT department.

There was a further assumption that employees would send in their best practices and would seek out the captured knowledge and use it. But of course, in many organizations people did not readily submit knowledge nor were they inclined to take it out of the warehouse. Seeing this, some organizations determined they would have to incentivize employees to get them to use the knowledge. Lots of schemes were put in place, for example, one organization offered frequent flyer points for putting best practices in the database. British Petroleum required teams to go through the database for best practices before starting a new project. They checked a box in the project plan to prove they had reviewed the best practice ideas. For the most part, these databases, even with incentives in place, did not produce much improvement. However, in a few organizations, notably Texas Instruments (TI) Ford Motor Company, they were very successful.

Texas Instruments became an early poster child for KM. TI CEO, Jerry Junkins, is reported to have said, "We cannot tolerate having world-class performance next to mediocre performance, just because we don't have a method to implement best practices." TI shared best practices across 13 wafer fabrication plants, building a repository in Lotus Notes. They developed a network of 150 facilitators whose task was to identify and then write up best practices from across the plants. The facilitators (using 10-50% of their time) also held ShareFairs to promote the best practices they accumulated. TI had a team of fifteen people in the central office who categorized the best practices, brought in best practices from other manufacturing companies to benchmark against, and helped the plants assess their current performance vs. the best. For TI this effort greatly reduced cycle times and performance variability, which reportedly saved $500 million in direct costs and eliminated the need for building a new plant. TI's slogan for KM became, "One free fab plant."

Ford Motor Company was another great example, saving millions of dollars by sharing manufacturing best practices between plants. For example, if a way to mount the bumper on a car 15 seconds faster was discovered in Germany, the factories that made the same car in ten other countries, could do it exactly same way. Given that 200 cars rolled off the manufacturing floor each day in each plant, that was a lot of time saved. Time, which was easily translated into dollars. Each plant had 5-10 production engineers who were responsible for productivity improvement in a section of the plant. The production engineers from all the plants met quarterly at one of the plants, to address problems and tour that plant. Each plant had one Focal Point who was responsible for entering that plant's useful practices into a database as well as taking up practices from other plants. A practice could only be entered if it had already shown the dollar savings in the originating plant. Each practice entered was sent to every plant, typically 5-8 processes per week. A response was required from each plant as to whether or not that plant would implement each of the practices, and if not, why not. Overall each plant was required to reduce cost each year by 5%, assuming the plant manager wanted to keep his/her job – so the practices were taken seriously. On average 40% of the required cost reduction came from practice replication. Management carefully tracked how many practices a plant sent in and how many practices each plant implemented. Over a period of 6-7 years, Ford saved $855 million from its best practices program.

This success of best practices was limited to places where:

- the work was repeatable, standardized and measurable

- management closely track who was sending in and taking up practices.

- there was a process in place to bring users together periodically to build trust in other's capability

- there were roles that were accountable for identifying and distributing the practices.

In organizations that simply built databases and expected potential users to participate, best practice repositories did not work well. In those places users then, pretty much did what we do now. They went online only when they needed to find the answer to a specific question or problem. They did not tend to just go into the repository to check if there were any new practices. Employees faced the additional difficulty that the search engines in the nineties were not very sophisticated, which made search time consuming and not very satisfying. As documents were added to the databases, they just kept accumulating, and there was often not a way for the searchers to know which document was newer or more relevant to their situation. Taxonomies were also in their infancy adding to the difficulty in finding documents.

Having spent thousands of dollars on repositories, with little return on investment, in many companies, management became disillusioned with knowledge management. We began to hear that knowledge management was dead. It had not lived up to its promise.

Some of the assumptions that were made about leveraging explicit knowledge in the first era were incorrect, others were correct, but were limited to one kind of knowledge - explicit knowledge, knowledge that could be documented. Table 1, lists those that were correct, partially correct and incorrect.

Correct	Partially Correct	Incorrect
knowledge is a critical organizational asset - This has turned out to be correct. An ever-growing number of organizations, recognize that knowledge is their primary product.	**knowledge can be managed** – This is still up for debate. Even what it means to manage knowledge is questionable. What is clear is that leaders need to think seriously about how knowledge flows within their organization as well as externally, to and from customers and suppliers.	**knowledge is stable -** knowledge changes continually. Ideas identified as best practice today, will be greatly improved tomorrow. Often by the time a practice gets written down, it has already been improved somewhere in the field.
	Employees will seek out and use practices that experts identify as "best practice" – employees will seek out knowledge when they have a need for it in front of them. Employees are proud of their own knowledge that has been learned through years of experience. To be the recipient of the knowledge that some unknown expert has declared as "best", challenges their sense of competence.	**There is a best way to accomplish any task.** Like the issue of stability, how to accomplish a task or even what tasks need to be accomplished is an ever-changing landscape. Best practice is a moving target.
	Just "connect people to content" Content is a necessary step, but falls short of being sufficient to leverage an organization's knowledge, much of which is only in people's heads and is growing daily as employees' experience grows.	**All the knowledge needed to do an effective job can be put into a written format.** A great deal of the basic knowledge about how to do a job can be written down, but unless you are talking about making a McDonald's hamburger, the complexity in today's jobs are learned through experience and with the help of peers.

Table 2-1. Leveraging Explicit Knowledge Assumptions

Leveraging Experiential Knowledge - Era 2

So, knowledge management was dead, or at least its reputation was badly tarnished. Then sometime around 2000 organizations began to think about knowledge in a new way and Leveraging Experiential Knowledge (the middle bar in my diagram) breathed new life and capability into knowledge management.

There was a growing recognition that those on the front-line had critical knowledge that was not being captured by the experts. If I had not known that before, my work with the U.S. Army's first Community of Practice, CompanyCommand (Dixon, Allen, Burgess & Kilner 2005) confirmed that for me. For example, the war in Iraq was changing so fast that there was no time for what was being learned on the battleground to be vetted, then turned into doctrine and finally be sent back out to the troops. What saved lives and won battles was the immediate exchange of knowledge among those on the frontline. It was not only on the battlefield that the need for the immediate exchange began to manifest itself. In many rapidly changing industries (e.g., technology, pharmaceutical, intelligence) it was the front-line that had the ground truth.

Organizations began to recognize that they had only been supporting explicit knowledge, that is, knowledge that could be written down. They had disregarded two other kinds of knowledge that were critical to organizational success, implicit and tacit knowledge. Implicit knowledge is "know how" that is learned through experience. When workers are asked questions about the "know how" that they have gained through their own mistakes and successes, they are able to answer those questions. In other words, front-line workers can take advantage of what others have learned without having to learn it for themselves. For example, insights about a difficult client or shortcuts to use in fixing a troublesome machine. But note these are context specific questions, they are not the best practice developed in the first era which by definition needed to apply to many situations. In era two, the asker is asking about a specific client that has a unique set of characteristics or a specific machine that has a repair history that must be taken into account. In the past, such questions were asked by walking down the hall to talk with an experienced colleague, but in organizations where workers were increasingly spread across the country how does implicit knowledge get shared?

The answer came from Etienne Wenger in his book Communities of Practice (1998). That book both gave communities their name and explained how "know how" or implicit knowledge moves from person to person within a social community. The awareness that communities, rather than just individuals, were sources of learning, came out of the anthropological studies that Wenger and his colleague Jean Lave (1991) initially conducted. They studied how participation in conversations among Yucatec midwives, tailors in West Africa, and even alcoholics attending AA meetings were able to gain greater expertise by interacting with peers. These were communities that arose spontaneously because the people that came together needed to grow their knowledge about a specific topic or skill.

The idea of Communities of Practice came at just the right time for organizations, because the World Wide Web and the technology that followed, made online communities possible. Given this new and broader understanding of the importance of implicit knowledge, organizations began to build COPs to provide a way for workers to ask questions and receive answers on a just-in-time basis and thus keep fast-changing knowledge up-to-date. The great advantage of having a large network was that if you had a specific situation, even though it might be rare in your division, somebody else in the world had experienced that same situation and could advise you.

Initially, organizations followed Wenger's thinking and allowed communities to form spontaneously. But within a few years, most organizations were primarily supporting communities that were related to their strategic interest. These organizations appointed online community managers, and often even put the community in charge of the training and development of that discipline. Another type of community, Communities of Interest were formed in some organizations by people who shared a common passion or interest, for example, language communities, or employees interested in a specific computer language. Frequently organizations provided online space for these extra-curricular communities but did not provide resources. By 2005 nearly every Fortune 500 Company had established Communities of Practice, acknowledging that context-specific knowledge needs to be continually exchanged because workers are continually learning from doing their work.

Organizations also became interested in Tacit knowledge during the second era. Tacit knowledge is recognizable as the familiar tasks we do that we don't even have to think about how we do them, for example, riding a bike, kneading bread, playing piano, or even hitting a nail with a hammer. In an organizational sense, tacit knowledge is the deep expertise that makes one speaker engaging while another is uninteresting; that makes a doctor an exceptional diagnostician; or a world-renowned conductor uniquely able to pull beautiful music out of an orchestra. Like implicit knowledge, tacit knowledge is gained through experience, but it is knowledge that is so well learned that an expert has difficulty articulating it. The idea that we hold tacit knowledge is attributed to Michael Polanyi, a chemist and philosopher of the 1950s. In his book The Tacit Dimension (1966) he says, "We can know more than we can tell."

Tacit knowledge is extremely valuable to organizations, yet has been difficult for organizations to figure out how to deal with it. There are two issues related to tacit knowledge; one is how to make use of the tacit knowledge of experts to solve a difficult problem. The second issue for organizations is how to transfer the tacit knowledge of their experts to others. An example of the first is the way the EU countries reduced the deaths that occurred at football matches in Europe. Too frequently the football matches end in death or injury of fans, often from fights and as often from trampling or suffocation. After such a tragedy, there was sometimes an investigation by the government which ended in firing the police chief but did not seem to result in lessons about how to make such events safer. In 2005 the Netherlands Police Academy suggested to the EU Police Cooperation Working Party that the police from all the EU countries begin to conduct Peer Review Evaluations. This was agreed to, and for three years such evaluations were conducted. Evaluation is the wrong word in our language because these reviews were conducted only at the request of the commander when a football match was to be held at home. A team of six, made up of four police chiefs (experts) from other countries and two researchers, would travel to the city where the match was being held, arriving on the day before the match. The host commander would have a list of observations that would be helpful to him. Using the list the commander and the team would make a plan. The day of the match the team, in pairs, would observe and interview according to the plan and on the day after the match, the team would meet to discuss their observations and prepare a draft report. In the weeks following, the report would be finalized and sent to the commander for his use. He could share it with others or keep it private, although most choose to share it with their officers and many with the whole community. Twenty evaluations were conducted over a three-year period. An EU manual on crowd safety resulted from the evaluations as well as the ideas being embedded in training programs. I interviewed one of the initiators of this transfer of tacit knowledge. Proudly he informed me that there had not been a football death in the EU in over 3 years. This is an example of police chiefs using their combined tacit knowledge to address a critical issue.

Examples of the second issue, helping others become more expert themselves, have included shadowing and personal coaching which have been used to increase the expertise of management consultants and sales people (Leonard, Swap &Barton 2015.) NASA has used storytelling effectively, gathering aspiring astronauts in the library to listen to the stories of celebrated astronauts and to question them. 3M has done something similar when a plant manager is nearing retirement. 3M gathers people who are one level down to listen to the pending retiree talk about the difficult challenges he or she faced, and to ask questions about the details. The World Bank uses a method they call Master Classes where, much like a master class for violinists or vocalists, a renowned expert challenges "nexperts" (those near to being an expert) to solve cases from the expert's work history.

One of the apocryphal stories about transferring tacit knowledge was written by Julian Orr, an anthropology doctoral student at Stanford, who was looking for a topic for his dissertation. Being in Silicon Valley, he decided to study how copy repair technicians went about their work of diagnosing and solving the problems of the machines they were trying to repair. Using his ethnographic skills, Orr lived with a team of technicians for six months, going on repair calls, on trips to the warehouse to pick up parts, etc. One of his insights was that tacit knowledge was being transferred when the technicians, in a geographic area, were gathered at a regular place for lunch. Typically, a technician, often a younger member, would start talking about a repair he or she had been working on but had not been able to figure out. The story would remind the more experienced technicians of similar difficult repairs and of how they had solved those problems. By the end of the lunch, the technician that had initiated the discussion would go away happy, not with the problem solved, but with some new possibilities that might lead to an answer. The experienced technicians were not solving the problem for the newer technician but through their stories were recounting how they go about solving that kind of problem – sharing their tacit knowledge of problem-solving.

What made this story apocryphal was that when Orr's dissertation (Talking About Machines, 1996) appeared in print, Xerox managers were aghast that technicians were meeting to learn from each other. At that time, Xerox was a company celebrated for its excellent training as well as for its comprehensive manuals full of decision trees to address any possible repair problem. Yet Orr discovered that all across the country, repair technicians were meeting with each other to talk about how they went about solving problems that were not in the training or repair manuals. At first the managers said the meetings had to stop - after all who knows what incorrect information these non-trainers were telling others. But over time the managers came to realize that they couldn't put the tacit knowledge in the manuals so rescinded the order to stop meeting. It is interesting to note that all of these efforts to help others gain the tacit knowledge of an expert are face-to-face events.

There were other ways that knowledge in this era began to be shared that also were not online forms. My book Common Knowledge (2000) illustrated the many different knowledge management processes through which teams and projects could share their knowledge. For example, I wrote about the US Army practice of conducting After Action Reviews (AARs) after every patrol, battle reconnaissance, troop movement, etc. to promote continuous learning in teams and projects. The findings from the AARS that applied to other units, were forwarded to the Center for Army Lessons Learned so that what was being learned in the field could be continually updated. NASA picked up the idea of AARs and changed the name to "Pause and Learn." British Petroleum also picked up AARs from the Army and used it extensively as have many other organizations. What began to be understood was that for a team to share its knowledge with others, it first had to figure out for itself what it had learned. That only happened if the group had come together to reflect on the actions they had taken individually and collectively, what results that produced, and what that meant for going forward.

In that book I also wrote about a process that originated with British Petroleum, they called, Peer Assist. As an example, when a refinery or an exploration team was ready to begin a project, they first brought together 5-7 people who had recently been involved in similar projects, often from across the world, to get their counsel to make sure they were starting with the latest knowledge from the field.

There are numerous other second era KM practices, 1) Knowledge Planning that helps teams anticipate what knowledge they will need and what knowledge they hope to learn from a task. 2) Sharefairs and 3) Retrospects that allow a project to share what it has accomplished as well as the mistakes it made; 4) Knowledge Jams, 5) Social Network Analysis, 6) knowledge audits, etc.

The Analogy for the first era was the warehouse. The analogy for the second era was the network where exchange is reciprocal. The assumption being that each person in the network is at times both an originator of knowledge that is shared with others and a recipient of others' knowledge. This reciprocal exchange reduced much of the resistance to accepting the practices of others that occurred in the first era.

What KM Learned in the Second Era:

- People on the front-line have ground truth (implicit knowledge) that they can learn from each other. This knowledge changes too fast to go through a vetting process, so it is up to CoP members to correct the mistakes of other members, which they do effectively. The concern that front-line employees will provide incorrect knowledge has largely disappeared.

- KM works best when the exchange of knowledge is reciprocal, everyone at all levels in an organization is learning and has knowledge to contribute

- Individuals have knowledge but that knowledge is created, grows and moves within a social community

- Teams and projects do not have complete and accurate knowledge to transfer to others until team members have taken the time to reflect together about what they have learned

- Learning tacit knowledge from others is time-consuming and requires face-to-face interaction

In many ways, the second era was the golden age of KM. But around 2010 some of the downsides of the second era began to be recognized.

- Leveraging Experiential Knowledge was largely focused on the front-line. Middle management, for the most part, was ignored, as was senior management. There were few processes for middle or senior managers to learn with and from each other or through reflection or transfer processes. Managers saw their KM responsibility as limited to supporting KM for the front-line, but did not see it as useful for themselves.

- One of the questions that management has struggled with in Leveraging Experiential Knowledge was how much control they should exert over communities, reflection sessions, and transfer events. For example, Should reports from AARs be sent up the chain of command and if so what would the impact be on candid reflection? Should managers establish a community's goals in exchange for support? How far can a peer exchange, that is inherently informal, be formalized before it loses its value? Although clear-cut answers to these questions did not emerge during the second era, a movement in the direction of reduced management control over content became evident.

- Network exchanges successfully moved knowledge between peers, those at roughly the same level in the organization - lateral transfer. However, there was little flow between hierarchical levels, for example, between managers and front-line workers, which precluded different levels from taking the knowledge of other levels into account.

- The knowledge that was exchanged was primarily about the tactical level of work. The strategic level was not addressed within Leveraging Experiential Knowledge. A team or project could use KM processes to improve how they were meeting their goals, but if the goals themselves were in the wrong direction, the practices of the second era provided no way to find that out.

Before turning to the third era, it is important to note that during the second era, KM's thinking about the first era did not stand still, improvements continued to be made in managing explicit knowledge. Chief among those was greatly improved search capability, often based on Google's algorithms. Also, taxonomies (Lambe 2007) became much more sophisticated and useful, and wiki's supplemented, and in some cases replaced, repositories as a means to retain knowledge. All of these advances made finding documents a much more pleasant and effective experience.

Leveraging Collective Knowledge - Era 3

I lived through the first two eras, thus have some confidence in the summations I wrote for each. For part three, we are still all in the midst of the journey and dealing with changes as they arise. It is harder to get a perspective on a moving target than it is to look backward, but here goes.

Let me first list a few of the changes that are impacting knowledge management practice. As in the previous two eras, some changes are brought about by advances in technology, but others are broader changes in society, and yet others are related to how organizations are transforming their management and governance practices. All of these changes directly or indirectly impact how we think about and implement knowledge management

- The societal erosion of cognitive authority

- The use of teams to get work done

- Work that is increasingly distributed or virtual

- The incorporation of knowledge management into other organizational functions

The Social Erosion of Cognitive Authority

I want to start with the broadest and perhaps most elusive of the changes in the third era, the societal erosion of cognitive authority. This phenomenon is not new, but it has certainly been accelerating, as well as gaining greater media attention. Cognitive erosion does imply an erosion of the legitimate right of those in positions of authority to make decisions for the benefit of the whole. Rather, it is a growing lack of confidence that, on their own, those in positions of authority are competent to do so – a questioning of the extent of their capability, knowledge and perhaps most in important, values.

Within organizations and more generally in society, the assumption that those in positions of authority have some understanding or capability that the rest of us lack - that they have knowledge we can trust, is being questioned. We have certainly had adequate justification for our disappointment with those in authority; in medicine - the awareness of an astounding number of medical errors, as well as, the pricing practices of pharmaceuticals; in religion - the sex scandals in the Catholic Church; in politics - senators who break the public trust to enhance their own wealth; in social media – the reports of false stories and fake news and more recently the sexual abuse of women.

Within the field of management, there have been CEOs whose actions have demonstrated that they have neither the interest of stockholders nor employees at heart. We have paid CEOs huge salaries, justified in large part by the premise that they possessed unique knowledge that the rest of us did not have – a belief in the hero leader who could make a difference to an organization's success. Since around 2010 that assumption has more and more been called into question. Recently, Winterkorn, the CEO of Volkswagen who resigned over the falsification of the emission controls (2015); John Stumpf, CEO of Wells Fargo, who was forced to resign for encouraging the opening of false savings and checking accounts (2016); the Penn State sexual abuse scandal perpetrated by Sandusky and then covered up by Spanier, the University president, and Curley, the Athletic Director (2011). As early as 2008 we learned about Bernie Madoff (Cohmad Securities Corp), Ken Lay (Enron) in 2002, and Bernard Ebbers (WorldCom) in 2001, as well as a host of others who have demonstrated that unchecked power corrupts. It is perhaps unnecessary to say that this is a knowledge management issue. It is about who has access to what knowledge and it is about whether the organizational culture is one in which employees are free to speak up about what is happening – both are issues of transparency.

In response to the erosion of cognitive authority in the third era, we are seeing more talk about the need for transparency at the top of an organization, which has led to the inclusion of organizational members in discussions of policy and strategy. A number of recent books have described organizations that extoll their transparency and inclusion. The book Joy, Inc., (2013) written by CEO Richard Sheridan, describes Menlo Innovations, an organization that has no hierarchy, rather, a number of conversational practices, e.g., regular morning meetings, team conversations with customers, etc. The Conversational Firm by Catherine Turco (2016) chronicles the practices of an organization (unnamed) where all topics of management and strategy are widely and vociferously discussed through the internal internet as well as through the periodic convening of town hall type meetings. An Everyone Culture, by Robert Kegan and Lisa Laskow Lahey (2016), describe three organizations, Bridgewater, Decurion and Next Jump, that are transparent and that use conversational formats, at all levels, to facilitate that transparency. And of course, we already knew about Gore and Morning Star. Gore has long had teams organized around self-selected opportunities and leaders who emerge organically. Morning Star practices self-management where employees' decisions about what they will work on are determined by their commitments to others, rather than on management. You could probably add to this list – it is growing.

KM has begun to play a growing role in organizational transparency. In the first and second eras, KM primarily designed and employed KM practices to support a strategy that was designed by those at the top of the organization. Typically, KM was in the service of cost cutting and time-saving. KM professionals had little interaction with the executive suite, looking to them for support, but not expecting them to make use of KM processes themselves. In the third era KM professionals have become more aware that transparency is necessary if organizations are going to leverage the collective knowledge fully, and have begun to add practices to their repertoire that do so.

"Collective knowledge" is not a new term to knowledge management, but in the past, it has been used in an additive sense, as in "all the knowledge an organization has." In the third era, it is being used in a quite different sense - to mean the knowledge that is derived from the confluence of diverse perspectives and data from across an organization and that is brought to bear on important organizational issues. But unlike the hierarchical process of passing everyone's ideas and data up the chain of command to someone at the top who would then make sense of them, with leveraging collective knowledge, the sensemaking is done jointly by those who hold those many perspectives and who own the data. It is joint sensemaking that is a hallmark of Leveraging Collective Knowledge.

Many online tools have appeared during the third era, including crowd sourcing, idea jams, prediction markets, information markets, decision markets, idea futures, event derivatives, and virtual markets. There are more sophisticated conference tools, for example, Skype, Zoom, Google Hangout, etc. that allow groups to not only hear but see each other, greatly facilitating the co-creation of knowledge. And conference tools that allow members of an online discussion to break into smaller groups for more in-depth conversation; Go to Meeting among them. And most important there are the many face-to-face meeting formats, knowledge cafés, appreciative inquiry, unconferences, etc. that are making leveraging collective knowledge more possible.

The Use of Teams to Get Work Done

The growing use of teams to get the work of organizations done has changed the way knowledge moves within an organization as well as the way knowledge is created. Teams have become the building blocks of organizations. They are the source of learning because they have greater autonomy to respond to customer requirements and to invent new solutions.

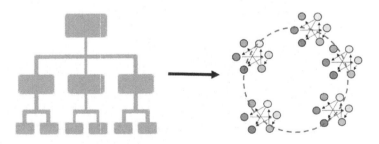

Figure 2-2. From a Structure Based on Hierarchy to a Structure Based on a Network of Teams

The 2016 Deloitte Human Capital Trends survey claimed that the new structure, which they referenced as a "network of teams," has shaken the foundation of organizational structure. Leading thinkers like McChrystal's (2015) Team of Teams, Edmondson's (2012) Teaming, and Hackman's (2011) Collaborative Intelligence have heralded and detailed this change. Google's four-year, in-depth study of their own teams is an indication of how serious organizations are taking this shift to teams (Delizonna, 2017).

Work being accomplished primarily by teams rather than individuals is significant for knowledge management. The movement to the network of teams is even more significant. I suggest five knowledge management implications of this movement below:

1. *The flow of knowledge within a team.* Teams are where organizational strategy is turned into action. A team's reflections on the outcomes of its actions serves to inform new action – which is the definition of learning (Dixon, 1999). Teams have become the unit of knowledge creation within organizations. There are KM strategies from the second era that have proven even more important in the third era, for example, Knowledge Planning that is used at the beginning of a task to help teams anticipate what knowledge it will need to do a task, as well as, what knowledge it plans to learn from doing a task; After Action Reviews, which provide a standardized process for a team to reflect on what it has learned. Also, technology has provided online team spaces like Slack and Yammer that increase team member coordination and collaboration. These spaces require KM professionals to guide team members in making them work. By the third era, we have realized that just putting a tool online is not enough.

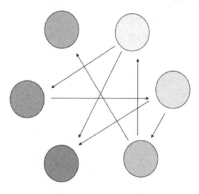

Figure 2-3. The Flow of Knowledge Within a Team

The concept of Working Out Loud has become important in the third era; creating greater transparency and a new kind of collaboration. In the second era, collaboration meant a team member offering others advice to address a problem or question. In the third era, the meaning of collaboration has broadened to include team members building on each other's ideas and incorporating diverse ideas into their work. Making work visible has expanded knowledge collection and invited a diversity of inputs. Rather than being a time out, conversation now occurs within the work stream and then becomes a project artifact that builds the knowledge base for the next project. Team members offer a range of feedback on the work of others, including inputs, agreement, appreciative comments, likes, etc. to keep project momentum going. Knowledge management professionals not only provide the tools for Working Out Loud, but have the responsibility for encouraging it, offering training for it, and just-in-time coaching for constantly arising questions a new learner has.

2. *The flow of knowledge between a team and its customers.* There are three types of customer knowledge 1) knowledge about customers, 2) knowledge for customers and 3) knowledge from customers. There is a great deal of software for all three types of customer knowledge, e.g., salesforce, Freshdesk, online customer communities. It is probably knowledge from customers that KM is most concerned with because customer knowledge allows a team to learn what's working, what isn't working, and what problems need to be addressed. Many KM professionals have become joint KM/Agile professionals because Agile is so closely aligned with KM philosophically, including having built-in processes for on-going interaction with customers.

3. *The flow of knowledge between teams.* Knowledge needs to flow between teams in a "network of teams" to coordinate the work of the organizations, given the reduction in hierarchy that the increased use of teams brings with it. Even the US Army has been pushing decisions down to Platoons and Companies. General Stanley McChrystal, (2015) as Task Force Commander in Iraq and Afghanistan, built within his Task Force a decentralized organization he called a "team of teams." By pushing down power and decision-making, he allowed teams to adapt quickly to changing events on the ground and come up with innovate solutions that could not have come from a top-down approach. He explains that after 9/11 Al Qaeda became a network and to deal with a networked Al Qaeda, the U.S. Army had to reshape itself into a network as well. McCrystal created a task force of representatives from each team to quickly assemble what was learned in the field. He explains that the relationship between task force members resembles a single team - a single interconnected mind.

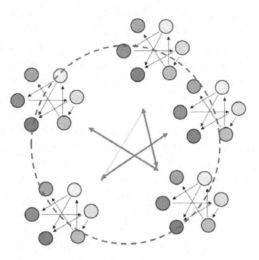

Figure 2-4. The Flow of Knowledge Between Teams

Many KM approaches that were developed and introduced in the second era were only minimally employed by organizations. But in the third era they have become critical to moving knowledge between teams, for example, Peer Assist that transfers knowledge from a team that has gained expertise in an area, to a team with less expertise in that area; Retrospects that bring representatives from different teams together to transfer what has been learned from a project; Share Fairs that display breakthrough ideas, often in technical areas.

A practice that was widely implemented in the second era was CoPs which provided a way for peers within the same discipline to share knowledge through Q&A. In the third era, there is a new CoP capability, one that facilitates the sharing of knowledge between communities, as well as the co-creation of knowledge. Wenger-Trayner (Wenger-Trayner, Fenton-O'Creevy, Hutchinson, Kubiak, & Wenger-Trayner, Eds. 2014) has labeled this flow of knowledge between communities and organizations as Landscapes of Practice – the convening of communities to address difficult issues.

A network of teams is a new organizational structure and thus demands a new way to think about KM. As KM professionals, we have the task of continuing to invent new processes that both create and move knowledge within a network of teams.

4. *The flow of knowledge from teams to the top of the organization to inform strategy.* Technology has provided many avenues for members of an organization to add their voices to the organizational strategy,

including the ideas mentioned earlier, e.g., crowd sourcing, idea jams and prediction markets. Organizations are also employing digital information centers, analytics dashboards, and visualization techniques that have largely replaced annual employee surveys. These tools still assume the responder is an individual rather than a team. It will be interesting to see how such online tools can accommodate ideas emanating from teams.

In the past, we have seen management periodically form task teams or tiger teams to address a difficult issue. Such teams then report their findings to management who make sense of the findings and take action based on them. But with a network of teams, the sensemaking is done between teams, not to the exclusion of the management team, but with a greater sense of equivalence.

5. *The flow of knowledge from the top of the organization to teams to inform teams' actions.* Leading-edge organizations have come to understand that in an age of increasingly complex organizational issues, leaders cannot be expected to have all the answers. The task of leaders becomes convening the conversations that can come up with new answers. Even long-established organizations have begun taking advantage of ways to bring the whole organization to bear on strategic issues. Leaders are calling upon KM professionals to convene groups in a variety of conversational formats to address organizational issues.

An example of leveraging collective knowledge was NASA's response to the cancellation of Constellation, the replacement for the Shuttle, that the ten NASA centers had been working on for five years at a cost of nine billion dollars. Lengyel, who headed NASA's Risk and Knowledge Management Program, needed a knowledge capture strategy that would provide direction over the next year as the program shut down. The capture strategy needed to include:

- how to identify the most critical knowledge to be retained
- effective methodologies for capturing knowledge
- how the captured knowledge should be formatted so it would be most useful to other parts of NASA or to the commercial companies that might eventually use it
- effective knowledge transfer techniques for a wide range of explicit and tacit knowledge
- an estimate of the potential cost of capturing and storing five years of work
- a way to prepare engineers with the skills to effectively capture and then transfer what they have learned.

Rather than designing a capture program himself, Lengel chose to address that need by leveraging the collective knowledge in NASA's ten centers. He invited people from each of the ten centers who had worked on the Constellation program for a two-day meeting to develop a knowledge capture strategy jointly. Before arriving, each had been asked to work with local teams to construct a knowledge map that identified and prioritized the knowledge in their center's part of the Constellation project. The first afternoon of the meeting, following the usual introductions and welcomes, the group did a walk-around of their maps, each of which had been blown up to poster size. During their walk-around, which was formatted much like a poster session, they examined each other's maps and gained ideas about how they might revise or add to their own. The next day was a day-long knowledge café. Each café table addressed a different issue related to knowledge capture and transfer, with participants moving from table to table until they had engaged in all of the topics. By the following morning, the table facilitators had formulated a draft plan based on the table discussions. As the facilitators presented their draft, everyone in the room commented and improved upon what the facilitators offered, using software that enabled each person to use their own laptop to project their reactions and comments for everyone to see. Based on the comments and ensuing discussion a final plan was created. This meeting was an excellent example of leveraging collective knowledge and illustrates the three elements that need to be in place to make use of the knowledge that resides in the minds of those doing the work, 1) joint sensemaking, 2) cognitive diversity, and 3) organizational transparency.

KM professionals facilitate the use of collective knowledge by conducting comprehensive and frequent analyzes of what is being said through internal social media in order to identify issues (elephants in the room) that need to be addressed with collective knowledge and then making those analyzes available to senior leaders so they can convene the conversations to address them.

The Increased Use of Virtual Teams

With the increase in virtual teams, leadership is necessarily becoming less centralized, depending more on distributed leadership among team members. Tools like Slack, Yammer, Google Docs, and Dropbox, make distributed leadership more possible. Visual meeting rooms like Skype, Google Hangout, Go to Meeting and Zoom make team collaboration easier. KM professionals are charged with providing workshops, power users and just-in-time coaching to make these tools useful to team members.

Virtual teams are new for many managers and many are still struggling with how to lead a team that is distributed across the world. Approximately half (51%) of HR professionals in companies that use virtual teams, report that building team relations is an obstacle that prevents them from being successful (Minton-Eversole, 2012).

Research has shown that team tools assist with coordination but in order for team members to co-create knowledge and to solve problems, it is necessary for team members to have periodic in-person interaction which creates needed trust and relationships among team members. Organizations, like Cisco where teams meet face-to-face, 2-3 times a year, (Cisco (2007) ProQuest where the Research Solutions team meets for three days, three times a year, Adobe and WordPress where managers are given the responsibility to bring people together to create "personal equity" are making use of both advanced online tools and periodic face-to-face convening to leverage collective knowledge effectively Mulhern, 2012).

KM professionals are helping managers recognize both the benefits and limitations of team tools. And they are helping design and facilitate in-person team meetings.

The Incorporation of Knowledge Management into Other Organizational Functions

While the focus on knowledge in organizations has greatly increased, the term knowledge management may be disappearing. In many organizations those responsible for KM have new titles and the divisions in which they are located have new names. What is happening to KM may be similar to what happened to Quality after the 80s. Every company had a Quality department in the 80's but over time quality got incorporated into how work was done. The separate departments of quality went away, but not the concept. Perhaps that is what is starting to happen in the third era, knowledge has become too important to be a separate function, it is being incorporated into larger efforts such as:

- innovation,
- idea generation,
- project management,
- change management,
- talent management,
- customer intelligence,
- digital workplace,
- social business.

Ads for KM positions are now often jointly labeled as "KM and Communication," Agile/KM, Social Media/KM.

Summary of Tasks for KM Professionals in the Third Era

I've summarized the tasks of KM professionals in the third era here. I recognize that these tasks are very different from much of the past work of KM professionals, but that has been so with each category. For example, those who were focused on building knowledge repositories were unsettled by having to learn how to build and support communities of practice when Leveraging Experiential Knowledge became important.

- Support the internal use of social media (crowd sourcing, decision markets) in order to increase the cognitive diversity brought to difficult organizational challenges and to increase transparency across the organization.

- Provide support for the online tools of the third era, through workshops, coaching, and developing power users, acknowledging that the tools will not be used or used effectively without substantial support.

- Assist managers in understanding and using the tools and processes available to manage virtual teams (Skype, Zoom).

- Facilitate the processes that support work being accomplished through teams, the online tools and the face-to-face processes AARs, Retrospects, Knowledge Jams, etc.

- Facilitate the processes that support a network of teams, Peer assist, Retrospects, KM planning, etc.

- Conduct comprehensive and frequent analyzes of what is being said through social media. to identify issues (elephants in the room) that are challenges that need to be addressed. Make this analysis available to leadership.

- When the leadership task is to convene the conversation to address difficult challenges the organization is facing, help leadership design the meetings, retreats, or conferences so that they are conversations not presentations.

- Help managers and senior leaders find or build a community.

Just as all organizational knowledge cannot be thought of as explicit or experiential, not all knowledge can be thought of as collective. Collective knowledge is simply another type of knowledge that we, as knowledge professionals, are able to address under specific circumstances.

Summary

The chart at the beginning of this article depicts the three categories along the knowledge management journey that I have talked about. The direction of change from the first to the third era is:

- from collection to connection to conversation.

- from learning as an individual task to learning in community to learning in public.

- from the focus on the product of learning, (lessons learned) to the focus on the joint process of learning.

- from "need to know" to transparency.

- from management control of content to trust in the organizational community to provide insight

- from a focus on tactical to a focus on strategic knowledge

- an increasing level of complexity from the first to the third era.

The answers to the questions I started out to explore about the nature of knowledge, I have answered for each era in the following table.

	Leveraging Explicit Knowledge	Leveraging Experiential Knowledge	Leveraging Collective Knowledge
Nature of knowledge	Stable, explicit, proven by scientific experimentation	Dynamic, frequently changing, "know how"	Meaning is created, not discovered. There are multiple possible meanings for any set of input
Who has important knowledge	Subject matter experts	Frontline workers	People who are cognitively diverse from across the organization, customers, suppliers, externals
Who needs to make use of the knowledge	Frontline workers	Frontline workers	Frontline workers Middle Management Senior Management
Who controls the content	Management identifies and approves the content that will be disseminated	User control of content	The convener initiates the topic of conversation but does not control the content

	Leveraging Explicit Knowledge	Leveraging Experiential Knowledge	Leveraging Collective Knowledge
Process for transferring knowledge	Collection and dissemination of "best" practices through knowledge repositories	Peer to peer networks of frontline workers	Conversations are public and transparent. For knowledge integration to occur transparency must be present
How knowledge is created	Scientific study, evidence based	Reflection on experience – individually and in teams	Created in conversation among those who have relevant, diverse information about the issue

Table 2-2. The Thinking About the Nature of Knowledge in Each Era

ABOUT THE AUTHOR

I consider myself a Conversation Architect. I am the founder of Common Knowledge Associates, a management consulting firm that helps organizations create conversations where knowledge transfer/sharing happens, where new knowledge is created, and where innovation arises. I take Margaret Mead's words seriously, "Never doubt that a small group of thoughtful, committed citizens can change the world. Indeed, it is the only thing that ever has."

The knowledge that organizations need to address their most challenging issues **resides within their organizations,** but that knowledge is too often unavailable to them because their members perceive it is too risky to speak up. What I have been very successful at doing is providing leaders the practices that create a psychologically safe space as well as provide members the critical dialogue skills that ensure that all the knowledge that could critically influence critical outcomes is available.

Before founding Common Knowledge Associates in 2000, I was a Professor at the George Washington University for 15 years, and before that at the University of Texas, in Austin. I hold a Ph.D. in Administration with a minor in Sociology.

I have written eight books as well as over 50 articles that focus on how organizations learn. My books include Common Knowledge: How Companies Thrive by Sharing What They Know, CompanyCommand: Unleashing the Power of the Army Profession, Dialogue at Work, and The Organization Learning Cycle, My latest thinking is on my blog, "Conversation Matters" at nancydixonblog.com.

My clients have included, among others:

- **The Defense Intelligence Agency** where I taught dialogue skills to analytic teams to enable them to speak truth to power
- **The US Army** where I worked with the widely-acclaimed community, Company Command, to encourage speaking up online
- **NASA** where I facilitated strategy development meetings that made use of the knowledge from all ten NASA centers
- **The Centers for Medicare and Medicaid** where I designed convocations across hospitals to improve Medicare outcomes and reduce costs

I am a runner, a committed yoga practitioner, a mother of two and a grandmother of three. I have the privilege of living in one of the most exciting cities in the US, Austin Texas. My work takes me around the world and I love the travel. I have come to know China, Singapore, Hong Kong, England, the Netherlands, Sweden, and many parts of the African continent.

BIBLIOGRAPHY

Cisco (2007), Understanding and managing the mobile workforce, Available at: http://newsroom.cisco.com/dlls/2007/eKits/MobileWorkforce_071 807.pdf (accessed 4 September 2016).

Delizonna, L.D. High-Performing teams need psychological safety. Aug 24, 2017 HBR

Dixon, N. M. (1999). The organizational learning cycle: How we can learn collectively. Gower Publishing, Ltd.

Dixon, N. M. (2000). Common knowledge: How companies thrive by sharing what they know. Harvard Business School Press.

Dixon, N. M., Allen, N., Burgess, T., Kilner, P., & Schweitzer, S. (2005). CompanyCommand: Unleashing the power of the Army profession.

Drucker, P. F. (1994). Post-capitalist society. Routledge.

Edmondson, A. C. (2012). Teaming: How organizations learn, innovate, and compete in the knowledge economy. John Wiley & Sons.

Hackman, J. R. (2011). Collaborative intelligence: Using teams to solve hard problems. Berrett-Koehler Publishers.

Kegan, R., & Lahey, L. L. (2016). An everyone culture: Becoming a deliberately developmental organization. Harvard Business Review Press.

Lambe, P. (2007). Organising knowledge: taxonomies. Knowledge and Organisational Effectiveness. Chandos, Oxford.

Lave, J., & Wenger, E. (1991). Situated learning: Legitimate peripheral participation. Cambridge university press

Leonard, D., Swap, W. C., & Barton, G. (2015). Critical knowledge transfer: Tools for managing your company's deep smarts. Harvard Business Press.

McChrystal, G. S., Collins, T., Silverman, D., & Fussell, C. (2015). Team of teams: New rules of engagement for a complex world. Penguin.

Minton-Eversole, T. (2012). Virtual teams used most by global organizations, survey says. Society for Human Resource Management, 19, 157-190.

Mulhern, F. (2012) Engaging virtual employees: innovative approaches to fostering community. The Forum (2012).

Orr, J. E. (1996). Talking about machines: An ethnography of a modern job. Cornell University Press.

Polanyi, M. (2009). The tacit dimension. University of Chicago press.

Sheridan, R. (2013). Joy, Inc.: How we built a workplace people love. Penguin.

Trends, G. H. C. (2016). The new organization: Different by design.

Turco, C. J. (2016). The conversational firm: Rethinking bureaucracy in the age of social media. Columbia University Press.

Wenger, E. (1998). Communities of practice: Learning, meaning, and identity. Cambridge university press.

Wenger-Trayner, E., Fenton-O'Creevy, M., Hutchinson, S., Kubiak, C., & Wenger-Trayner, B. (Eds.). (2014). Learning in landscapes of practice: Boundaries, identity, and knowledgeability in practice-based learning. Routledge

Seek wisdom, not knowledge. Knowledge is of the past, wisdom is of the future.

~ Lumbee Proverb

.

PUTTING STORIES TO WORK: DISCOVER

ABOUT THE CHAPTER

The vast majority of business leaders are not business storytellers. Sure, they share stories when they get together with family and friends. We all do. Storytelling is a very human condition. But when communicating in business, most leaders rely solely on reasoning, argument and logic to get their message across and to try and inspire action. If they have given storytelling any thought at all, they are usually of the misguided view that sharing a real-life experience is a waste of time—it's not business-like. The majority of business leaders, however, haven't even considered the power of storytelling. They haven't realised why some of their peers are engaging communicators and others are not.

This chapter, which focusses on Story Discovery, comes from my book, *Putting Stories to Work: Mastering Business Storytelling.* Story discovery is the foundation of business storytelling. By developing a keen eye that can discern stories from story imposters, and the ability to notice the many stories that constantly swirl around you, you will put yourself in the best possible position to find and tell stories that engage, influence and inspire. With your stories in hand, you then need to learn how to remember them so they can be told off the cuff.

This chapter is:

Please cite as:

Callahan, S. (2018). Putting stories to work: Discover. In J. P. Girard & J. L. Girard (Eds.), *Knowledge management matters: Words of wisdom from leading practitioners* (49-71). Macon, GA: Sagology.

3

PUTTING STORIES TO WORK: DISCOVER

BY SHAWN CALLAHAN

One sunny Melbourne day I was sitting in an Italian restaurant with the CEO of Volunteer Fire Brigades Victoria. Our conversation turned to how his organisation was improving the way it worked. The CEO said: ' We're looking at developing a best-practice database'. Now just a mention of the phrase 'best-practice database' makes my insides churn: I've yet to see one work. But rather than just blurt out my opinion, I shared a story that popped into my mind. 'Best-practice databases are one way to go,' I said, 'but there are other options. Something came out of 9/11 that's a good lesson'.

When the attacks of September 11 happened, the US Federal Aviation Administration had to get 5000 planes out of the air as fast as it could. But such a mass grounding had never been done before. The normal procedures, the best practices, they just didn't apply. Frantic air traffic controllers simply guided planes onto the closest runways by phoning colleagues at other airfields to see if they had room. Afterwards, the FAA tried to analyse what had happened so it could update its rulebook. But to its credit, it quickly worked out that this would be pointless. It hadn't been carefully worded policies that had carried the day but rather the strength of the relationships between smart, purposeful people—people who trusted each other to make the right decisions. The FAA instead invested in making sure that air traffic controllers and other key airline workers stayed connected.

When I finished my story, the CEO just leant back and said, 'And we have one of the biggest networks of firefighters in the state. We need to be thinking of ways to connect them'.

I first came across the 9/11 story in a paper by management consultant Margaret Wheatley.[1] As soon as I discovered it I knew it was one I wanted to retell because it made a point I strongly believed in: an organisation's ability to respond to the unpredictable is largely a function of the strength of its relationships. But it was also a good story. Lives were at risk. There was a twist, a lesson. It was an event we all have strong memories of. And the story was simple enough to tell in a couple of minutes.

Now I didn't go into that meeting in the restaurant planning to tell that story. Rather, it was triggered by the conversation. And that can only happen if you have a repertoire of stories to tell.

So how do you discover good business stories? It all starts with the ability to spot a story, and the realisation that people often think they're telling a story when, in fact, they aren't.

Beware The Non-Story

Everyone is talking about stories these days: 'What's the story of our business?' 'What's the story of our product?' 'What's my personal story?' I even saw an advertisement in a shirt shop on Fifth Avenue in New York announcing the story of the shirts. But if you listen carefully, you'll discover that many people who purport to share a story are not actually sharing one at all. It's as if they think that if they are talking, they are telling a story. This is a big problem—you simply don't get the benefits of storytelling unless you are telling a bona fide story.

I remember talking to a CEO a while back about how he could use business storytelling to communicate his company's strategy. The CEO said, 'Shawn, that's what I do already. I tell the story of our company'. So I asked him to tell me that story, and this is essentially what he said: 'We're a leader in our industry both in market share and revenues. We have the very best people and we are setting the agenda. I'm extremely proud of the work they are doing. But most importantly, we listen to our customers and give them the very best service and products…' And on he went. When he'd finished, I said, 'With all due respect, what you've just shared is not a story. It's a series of assertions'. I explained the difference, and to the CEO's credit he was open to learning more about oral storytelling, beginning with the ability to spot stories.

Many people in business have trouble telling a story from an opinion. For example, in many of the fanciest bathrooms around the world, you will see the output of the beauty products company Aēsop. Not lost on me is the irony that Aesop was also the name of a clever Greek storyteller who was renowned for fables such as *The Tortoise and the Hare*, and who, as legend has it, was incredibly ugly. But anyway, go to the company's website and click on 'About Aēsop' to find 'The Aēsop Story', reproduced below. I've added some comments in italics.

Aesop was established in Melbourne in 1987. [*OK, this sounds like the beginning of a story.*] Our objective has always been to formulate skin, hair and body care products of the finest quality; we investigate widely to source plant-based and laboratory-made ingredients, and use only those with a proven record of safety and efficacy. [*Those are just assertions.*] In each of our unique stores, informed consultants are pleased to introduce our range and to guide your selections. [*Another assertion.*] Alongside our commercial activities, we explore and support the arts as an avenue through which to inspire, learn and communicate. [*Nothing like a story.*] We are headquartered in Melbourne, and have offices and stores in many parts of the world, including New York, London, Paris, Tokyo and Hong Kong. [*Nope, no story here.*][2]

Instead of a story, we are presented with a list of principles, a set of descriptions of the company, and some interesting facts. It's said that a fable is a fiction picturing the truth. But a list of facts rarely delivers any deep understanding. I think the Greek Aesop would have been disappointed.

How To Spot Stories

Many people know what a story is until they are asked to find or tell one. To accurately spot stories, you need to train your ears to differentiate them from opinions, viewpoints, statements of fact, and the many other things that aren't stories. This is an essential skill; without it, systematic and purposeful business storytelling is impossible. Our ability to spot stories is based on the simple fact that stories have structure, which is why Anecdote has developed a story spotting framework.

SPOTTING AN ORAL STORY

HAS A BUSINESS POINT = BUSINESS STORY

THE STORY SPOTTING FRAMEWORK

Before we go any further, let me just say that the story spotting framework is not an attempt to come up with a rigid definition of a story. Rather, it's merely a tool that will help leaders to identify useful stories. In that context, the framework is a simple device that allows you to quickly decide whether something you're hearing is a story or not. Now let me break it down for you.

Oral stories often begin with a time marker (denoted by the clock image). When you hear someone say, 'Just this week...' or 'The other day...' or 'In 1991...', it's likely they are starting a story. Of course, the fabled time marker is 'Once upon a time...', but let me tell you, avoid this phrase in business. It never goes down well.

Sometimes an oral story starts with a mention of place (place tag image); for example, 'We were in the boardroom and Bill walked in...' or 'At the crusher Sam heard the bell...'

Stories mostly begin with either a time marker or a place marker because they are always set in a particular time and place.

Connected events are the bare essentials of a story (events image). Stories describe something that happened, and discrete events provide the backbone of this. When you hear someone using linking phrases such as 'and then...', 'and after that...', 'but then...' or 'because of that...', there's a good chance you're hearing a story.

The creators of the animated sitcom *South Park*, Trey Parker and Matt Stone, warn fledgling animators that if two scenes are separated with 'and then...', the result is likely to be a boring story. However, if the scenes are connected with the equivalent of 'but...' and 'therefore...', things stay interesting. We like to hear how people face and then resolve problems. That said, the view that a story must have a protagonist who faces and then overcomes a challenge, a notion highly influenced by Hollywood, is too narrow for business storytelling. For example, stories about coincidences lack a hero or a challenge, yet they are clearly stories that people love to tell. The story-rich podcast *This American Life* once dedicated an entire episode to coincidence stories.[3]

Stories have people doing things, including talking (people image). If you hear someone's name followed by what they did, or if you hear dialogue, the odds are you're listening to a story. In fact, dialogue can only be delivered in a story—it's a real giveaway.

A story is also a promise to share something the audience doesn't know (wham image). To qualify as a story, there must be something in it that's unanticipated. It doesn't have to be a great insight, but the listeners should at least raise their eyebrows a little. That's what makes it story-worthy.

Lastly, to be a business story, a story must have a business point.

Fine-Tuning Your Ability to Notice Stories

Now that you know a practical way to detect stories, you need to fine-tune your radar to notice the best stories for retelling in a business context. While the story spotting framework will help you to find a story, it says very little about whether the story is a good one. As a general principle, there is a hierarchy of story impact that goes like this:

- A story *describes* what happened.
- A good story helps you *see* what happened.
- A great story helps you *feel* what happened.

Early in the 20th century, biologists observed how some animals learn how to notice a specific type of prey and become extremely good at finding it. For example, birds can detect a specific type of worm or beetle from quite a distance. Biologists call this a search image.[4] As a leader, you need to develop your own search image for stories.

The first thing to do is to take yourself to places where stories are told: head down to the office cafeteria, visit a local restaurant or diner, or join in those pop-up corridor conversations. You can also arrive early for a meeting to hear the general chitchat, or stay on after the formal part of the gathering ends. The informal parts of meetings really matter. An Australia-based medical supplier that has an office in the United States learned this first-hand. The guys in the US felt on the outer because whenever they had a teleconference, the communication equipment was only taken off mute when the meeting got down to business; they didn't get to take part in any of the chitchat. So the company made a small change to its teleconference procedures that allowed everyone to hear the informal conversations at both ends of a meeting. By doing so, it brought its people closer together.

Now listen to the conversations taking place, keeping an ear out for time markers—you'll be surprised at just how many stories begin with these. Notice the types of stories being told. How long are they? What are they about? Who features in them? Who are the heroes and who are the villains? Now notice how you respond to the stories. How do they make you feel? Do any give you a tingle of emotion? Keep a mental note of any stories that generate an emotion. These are the stories with power. As the late American author and poet Maya Angelou was often quoted as saying: 'People will forget what you said, people will forget what you did, but people will never forget how you made them feel'.

The inventor Steve Gass had been working on a safety brake for high-speed table saws that immediately stopped the saw on contact with human flesh. Steve had already tested his invention with human-flesh stand-ins such as hot dogs, and sure enough, each time he pushed the sausage at the saw blade, it stopped, leaving the meat without a scratch. But now, with the saw spinning at 10,000 RPM, it was time to test out his invention in the way that really mattered. Gass readied himself and, with a deep gulp, pushed an index finger into the whirring blade. The saw abruptly stopped. Gass saw that his finger was unharmed and exclaimed: 'It really works!'[5]

When I read this story, I knew immediately that it was relatable because it sent shivers up my spine and set the hairs on my arms on end. I then told it to my family, and just by the looks on their faces I knew it had had an impact.

Of course, while this is a good story, to be a good business story it must have a business point. The good news is that nearly any story can be turned into a business story. All you need to know is why you might tell it in a business context. In the case of the Steve Gass story, you might decide that it's about the importance of doing something remarkable to get the attention of your backers and your customers.

So as you discover stories, it's important to ask yourself the questions: 'What's the point of this story, and when might I tell it?' Once you work that out, then you have a good business story on your hands.

Getting back to noticing stories, so far we've only discussed stories that are told by other people. But it's also an idea to catch yourself sharing stories. Try to notice when you're sharing an experience and how your audience responds to it. This feedback will help you improve the next telling and it will give you an insight into whether the story resonates. Once your own stories become apparent, quickly decide whether they might make a good business point, and if they do then jot them down. Oral stories are ephemeral, like rain: catch them when they fall, before they evaporate. As you fine-tune your radar, you'll start to notice stories everywhere.

Rough Diamonds

After some practice in spotting stories with a business point, you will be ready for the next level of story noticing, which is the ability to spot stories that are not yet fully formed. These are rough diamonds that need cutting and polishing.

Ric Holland is the CEO of Melbourne City Mission, which devotes itself to helping vulnerable people, including the homeless. One of its programs, which is run in Melbourne's CBD, is called Gateway Reconnect. The program's volunteers work on the street, engaging with young people who are affected by homelessness.

One day a man who looked to be in his 40s, wearing a suit, approached some of the volunteers on King Street. 'Are you with the City Mission?' he asked them. When they said yes, he pulled out a small photo album filled with pictures and started to describe them: 'This is me and my wife. We got married 10 years ago. This one is of my two beautiful daughters. And this one here was a big day for me. I was off to my new job'. The volunteers discovered that the man had gone through the Gateway Reconnect program some 20 odd years ago, and he'd come back to say thanks and show the current volunteers the impact of their work.

This is more or less how Ric told me the story. He re-enacted how the man showed each photo in the album. It was moving. Then Ric said that on the day this happened, the volunteers went back to the office and said: 'We had a guy in a suit show us his photo album today. He went through the program 20 years ago and has done pretty well'. As you can see, the volunteers' telling of the story was a little undercooked. But Ric saw it as a rough diamond—it had potential. He asked lots of questions and eventually worked out the bigger story.

Ric's ability to see the potential in a story fragment is something that you'll develop over time as your story spotting skills progress. If you think there might be a bigger story behind something, ask a few questions. Perhaps you'll be surprised at what you discover.

Here's another example of a rough diamond. Back in the 1980s, Van Halen was the biggest rock act on the planet. They would roll into a city with nine 18-wheelers and assemble a stage the weight of a 747 jet. The demands made of the local promoter were extensive. The band even insisted that a bowl of M&Ms be provided backstage, but without any brown ones. When the band walked into their dressing room, they'd check if there were any brown M&Ms. If there were, they'd know that the promoter was not focused on the details of the gig and they'd order a full review of the staging to ensure it was safe.[6]

Now this story could be told to make a point about having good indicators in a complex job to ensure safety. I could imagine asking at the end of the story: 'What are our brown M&Ms?' So it clears the first hurdle of needing a business point. But this is a good little story for a couple of other reasons.

First, it's relatable. Nearly all of us know about rock bands from going to concerts and seeing them on TV, so we can easily picture something like this happening. We have plenty of our own experiences to draw on to bring this story to life. That means this story would work for a broad audience. Not all stories do. Imagine if, instead of the Van Halen anecdote, you told the story of a Xerox photocopier repairman and how he got an E053 error and started replacing the shorted dicrotrons which only created a 24-volt interlock problem. The majority of audiences would not be able to relate to this—not unless they happened to be Xerox photocopier repairers.[7] (By the way, this is a real example from ethnographer Julian Orr's classic book of storytelling and knowledge transfer, *Talking about Machines*. Orr showed in his study of photocopier repairmen that we tell stories to solve problems.)

The Xerox example might seem far-fetched, but I saw one leader tell a story about their Maserati and another tell one about Renaissance art collecting, which for most employees are equally unrelatable. Needless to say, in both cases the stories bombed.

The brown M&Ms story is also surprising. Who would have guessed that Van Halen's seemingly unreasonable request had such an important purpose. This story has a surprising twist, and audiences love surprises.

Then there are some story topics we are particularly drawn to: namely power, death, children's safety and sex. These four topics strike a chord with our lizard brains—paying close attention to these issues has ensured our species' survival, and as a result these topics make for sticky stories. Powerful people, for example, can make our lives a misery or a joy, so we've learned to keep an eye on them and as a result we are drawn to stories of such people. The Van Halen connection is that power comes in different flavours, including position, education, money, celebrity and beauty. Van Halen have celebrity power.

We've obviously also learned that it's good to try and avoid death, so we notice stories about death or near-death experiences. It explains why there are so many TV programs that feature murder. When we hear about a death, we want to know how it happened so we can archive that story and then do our best to avoid a similar fate. Our species survives because of children, so we are also hardwired to notice stories about children in danger. Think about how quickly a story about a child in harm's way goes to the top of the news cycle. And yes, we care about sex. Advertisers have known this forever. Though I have to say, this one is tricky to work into business storytelling.

These are just some of the features of stories that can help you tell the rough diamonds from the diamantés. In Chapter 5, I talk more about the characteristics that increase the likelihood of stories being remembered and retold.

* * *

The ability to spot stories is a curse as much as a blessing, because once you have this ability you start to see stories everywhere. If you're like me, you'll start counting the stories someone tells in a presentation, and when no stories are told you'll think to yourself: 'Man, this section is just not going to stick '. But spotting stories is *the* fundamental narrative intelligence you need to become a business storyteller. And this is not a passive exercise. The stories we find, and especially the ones we retell, change who we become. As the famed fantasy author Terry Pratchett once observed: 'People think that stories are shaped by people. In fact, it's the other way around'.[8] A story spotting ability will also help you guard against the many people who say they are telling the story of their product, company or project, when in fact they are not. Only those who tell actual stories will get the wonderful benefits of storytelling.

Where to Look for Stories

My 21-year-old daughter Alex stepped onto the stage to perform her song, an Adele classic. The audience was seated cabaret-style and the lights were low. Alex was two-thirds of the way through the song and we were all enjoying the performance when suddenly her microphone stopped working. She tapped it. Nothing. As the backing track continued to play, I could see concern drawing across her face. Then we saw a flash of movement from stage right. The MC sprinted across the stage to Alex and handed her his own microphone. It arrived just in time for Alex to take up the chorus, which she belted out with a wide grin. The crowd went wild, and when Alex had finished they gave her a standing ovation.

I wasn't thinking about storytelling during my daughter's performance. But when my family got together afterwards and talked about what had happened, it dawned on me that Alex's recovery on stage was a bit like what can happen with customer service: you can get a bigger, more positive reaction if you recover well from a mistake than after a flawless performance.

There are lots of places where you can find good business stories to tell: listening to other people tell stories; in descriptions of experiments; in books, movies and podcasts. And I cover all of these in this section. But your own stories should be at the top of the list. This involves reflecting on your experiences rather than letting life just wash over you. It means drawing connections between lived experience and business ideas—such as customer service.

Some might think it is inappropriate to share a personal story at work. There is, however, a significant benefit in telling a personal story to make a business point: your audience gets to know a little bit more about you as a person. When, as a leader, you tell a personal story, it humanises you. It allows your people to get a sense of what's important to you. This improves engagement, which is good for business.[9]

Your Own Stories

There are so many things happening around you, and your job is to notice them. A simple way to get started is to think about the things that have happened in the last 24 hours. Ask yourself if anything occurred that gave you an insight into your own character or contained a lesson. Jot down what you discover.

If you find a lack of interesting things in your vicinity, then you need to expand your horizons and go to where the action is. Business author Tom Peters calls this 'management by wandering around'.[10] Go to where decisions are made, where leaders gather and important meetings are held (when I worked for IBM, the monthly sales call was a great source of stories). Go wherever there's a crisis or people under pressure, or where new things are happening. Go wherever the quirky, eccentric mavericks hang out.

A few years ago I ran a public storytelling program at the University of London. Just before the workshop started, as I was looking out a window towards Russell Square, I noticed what looked like a Victorian-era garden shed. Out front were a couple of taxis and a group of people having morning tea. It was a cabbie shelter, where the drivers gathered when they took time off. If I had been a new cabbie, that would've been a great place to hear stories that would help me develop my own strategies for getting more fares, avoiding trouble and getting help when I needed it.

Taking excursions to where things are happening enables you to say things like: 'I was down at the factory and I could see there was an intense discussion happening between four managers in the middle of the floor…' Just the beginning of that story makes us want to know what happened. The story might end up being about a lesson that was learned, an organisational value that was reinforced or thwarted, an example of great leadership, or any one of a multitude of other possibilities. But the important thing is *you* saw it happening, so it's a story you can tell as your own.

Photographs

Have you ever been to a presentation where the speaker shows you interesting things they've taken photos of ? To me, this is always more interesting than a slick slide deck of dot point after dot point. Most of us have smartphones these days, which means we have a camera in our pocket. Whenever you see anything that's remarkable, snap a picture of it. Apart from reinforcing the incident so you can remember it, the photo can be included in your next presentation.

Sheenagh and I recently returned home from a holiday in Europe. We were keen to show our two daughters the photos from our trip, but we'd taken hundreds of them. Alex suggested we select a dozen photos that each triggered a story and create a slide show using those. It was a terrific suggestion. Not only did it save Alex and her sister Georgia from having to look at a lot of boring images, but the pair heard some cracking stories. It also taught me that images which show people doing something are much more evocative in terms of storytelling than static images of buildings or mountains. As it turns out, not all pictures tell a story—at least, not a good one.

Triggering Stories

Sometimes, finding good stories to tell is not enough. Sometimes you need to actively trigger new stories.

The family-owned Mars, Inc. is one of the largest food businesses in the world—in 2015 it generated more than US$30 billion in revenue.[11] The company has five core principles it holds dear, one of which is to take responsibility. A few years ago, company chairman John Mars attended a presentation at a factory in the rural Australian town of Wodonga. Part way through the session, one of the fluorescent lights above the boardroom table started to flicker annoyingly. Without a word, John stood up and left the room, returning a few minutes later with a stepladder. As the presentation continued, he climbed the ladder, removed the light, took the ladder back outside, then sat back down at the table and resumed listening to the presenter. The chairman did all that without any fanfare, but his actions spoke volumes. He demonstrated the taking of responsibility, reinforcing a key principle of the company. That story has since literally travelled the world: I heard it in a workshop I was running in New York.

This is story triggering: doing something remarkable that gets other people to tell a story.

Stories Other People Tell

People tell us stories all the time, and some will be worthy of retelling. In fact, a leader should encourage people to share their stories, a skill I call story listening. But before I talk about how to collect these stories by establishing the right conditions for them to be told, and by asking story-eliciting questions, here's something to keep in mind when you use someone else's story: it's wise to acknowledge where the story came from when you tell it. To do this, just say something like: 'Anna told me this the other day...' Referencing the source hardly diminishes the impact of the story. But more importantly, you avoid the embarrassment of being caught telling another person's story as if it was your own. I've seen this happen and it's not pretty.

Mark Schenk and I once went to a networking event which the master of ceremonies kicked off by telling a story. He began by saying he'd been at an airport recently and found himself sitting in the departure lounge beside an elderly woman who was quietly sobbing. As the MC continued, Mark felt that the story was familiar, so he googled it and found that it was a story making the rounds on the internet, about reaching out to strangers in need. The MC had purloined the anecdote and reshaped it as if it had happened to him.

Perhaps no-one else in the audience twigged to what was going on. And it was a good story which everyone enjoyed. But in a business setting, the word will eventually get out and your credibility will be undermined. If this happens, the next time you recount a story there will be a big question mark in everyone's minds as to whether it was borrowed too. So while it might be tempting, just don't do it. It's vital that your stories remain authentic and that you remain trustworthy.

A better strategy for the MC would 've been to say, 'I saw this story on Facebook recently and it really sums up my feelings about...', then tell the story. An even better strategy, of course, would've been for the MC to tell one of his own stories.

Conditions for Stories to Be Told

Sometimes you need to coax other people into telling their stories. For this to be effective, the conditions need to be just right for effective story listening to take place. It's partly to do with your attitude and partly a product of the environment.

In my work collecting stories in companies, I've found there are six conditions that help stories to be told:

1. *A caring listener.* You have to care about and be interested in the stories being told. People have a finely tuned sense of whether others care about what they are saying. If they detect disdain or boredom, they'll truncate their stories or just stop telling them altogether. So put on your listening hat.

2. *Free time.* Don't be in a hurry. Remember the last time you went on a long road trip with a friend or colleague? Remember the stories you heard? Stories seem to emerge when we are not under pressure or constrained by formality. For example, loose meeting agendas are more likely to encourage stories than highly structured ones.

3. *Common ground.* If someone doesn't think you will understand their story, or decides it's too much of an effort, they won't share it.

   I remember calling my brother Scott in Arizona back when he was a wine salesman (he's now VP of sales) and him telling me what a talented sales manager he had. I asked him to share an example of what this talented guy had done to earn his praise. Scott hesitated, then he started giving me high-level descriptions of the sales manager's attributes rather than a story. I finally realised that because I didn't share his wine sales knowledge, he thought I might not appreciate (or get) his stories. So I said, 'Just pretend I'm an experienced wine guy'. He then shared a great example of his sales manager's abilities. And his instincts were right: I didn't really understand it. Common knowledge is needed at some level before stories can be effectively shared.

4. *Stories.* Stories beget stories. One of the best ways to encourage someone to share a story is to tell one yourself.

   When I used to pick up my daughters after school, I would ask how their days had gone, whether anything interesting had happened, and their standard responses were often monosyllabic: 'Yep'; 'Nup'. In fact, the more questions I asked, the shorter were the answers. So I changed tack and rather than ask questions, I simply recounted something that had happened in my day. I'd launch into something like: 'I met a poet today. This morning I drove down to Fitzroy to run an anecdote circle for...' Almost immediately, my daughters would respond by describing one of their experiences from that day.

5. *Artefacts.* One of the most enjoyable projects I've ever done involved helping an energy company collect stories from its retiring network controller, Mike. His job was to keep tabs on the entire electricity grid and resolve problems as they happened, and his office was filled with maps, computer screens and whiteboards, all covered with notes and sketches. Storytelling was easy for Mike. He would grab a map of the grid and tell me the story of how a particular substation had gone down and how they'd fixed it. Mike retired before we finished the story collection, but he invited me to his home a couple of months later to finish the job. But this time, as we sat in his lounge room surrounded by family snaps and keepsakes from overseas trips, he struggled to tell me his work stories. And when he did share one, the detail wasn't as rich as in those he'd told in his office. It was as if the artefacts in his office had contained parts of the story. Since then, when I'm collecting stories from someone, I'll pick a place to do it that has artefacts to prompt them. Or if I'm running a workshop, I'll ask everyone to bring in one thing that's significant to them and then get them to explain why— that always brings great stories.

6. *Trust.* Sharing a story can reveal a lot about someone, so the storyteller needs to feel they are in a safe place, that they can trust the listener to treat the story with respect and not misuse or misrepresent it. If this trust is missing, the story will either not be told or it will lack important details.

These six conditions for storytelling came together for me on my first trip to Washington DC. As I mentioned at the end of *Putting Stories to Work: Mastering Business Storytelling* Chapter 1, a fellow storyteller, Paul Costello, had agreed to show me around the National Mall. Paul's work involved bringing the next leaders of Israel and Palestine together in Washington to get to know each other, and as part of that program he would tell the young envoys stories about the architecture and monuments in and around the National Mall. We started at the Willard Hotel: I heard how Martin Luther King wrote his 'I Have a Dream' speech in one of the hotel's rooms the day before the civil rights march, and that apocryphal story of Ulysses S. Grant taking meetings in the lobby. Paul then shared a story about the statue atop the Capitol building, how the figure started off as an Indian slave but was transformed into an Indian goddess. At the Vietnam Veterans Memorial I learned how the first incarnation of Maya Lin's masterpiece had been carved in mashed potatoes. Each place we visited sparked new stories, and they reminded me of old stories. All the conditions for stories to be told were met that day. It was the beginning of a new friendship.

Story-eliciting Questions

One of the essential skills for story listening is the ability to ask the right questions, and I'm always on the lookout for new ones to ask. So when I first came across *The Art of Powerful Questions*, I was excited about what the authors would suggest.[12] As it turned out, they proposed that there are some questions that are more powerful that others, and they depicted this hierarchy as a pyramid. At the top was 'why', on the next level down were 'what' and 'how', and at the bottom, suggesting they were the least-effective questions, were 'when' and 'where'. I was puzzled. From the perspective of eliciting stories, this was almost the opposite of what I had experienced.

Because stories are bound to a time and a place, the best questions take you to that moment in time or that place as quickly as possible. These are usually 'when' and 'where' questions. 'Why', 'how' and 'what' questions, on the other hand, tend to get you an opinion rather than a story.

For example, if you asked someone, ' Why did your project succeed?', the list of responses might include:

- We had a clear purpose.'
- 'There was great leadership sponsorship.'
- We had the funds we needed.'
- 'Our team was amazing.'

There would be no story in sight. If, however, you asked, 'When did you make the best progress in the project?', you would likely be told a story about when that happened. And from that story you would learn about the clear purpose, the talented team members, the funding and so on.

There are exceptions of course. One of my favourite story-eliciting questions is simply, 'What happened?' So if someone says something like, 'We had an amazing turnaround in the middle of the project', you jump in and ask, 'What happened?'

Here are five types of stories it's useful for a leader to have ready to tell, and some story-eliciting questions to help you find them. These questions come from an eBook I wrote with Mark Schenk called *Character Trumps Credentials*.[13]

1. Stories that show your character

    - What's one of the hardest choices you've ever had to make?
    - What three things have happened in your life that have shaped who you are today?

2. Stories that show you care

    - When have you put people before results?
    - When have you been surprised by what you truly care about?

3. Stories about purpose

- When has your purpose been clear and strong?
- Have you ever been part of a group that went beyond expectations because they believed so strongly in what they were doing?

4. Stories about lessons

- When have you said to yourself, 'I'll never do that again!'?
- What is one of the most important lessons you ever learned?

5. *Stories that inspire*

- Have you seen people become inspired to come from behind to win, or turn around a bad situation?
- When you are looking for inspiration, what moments do you reflect on?

Published Stories

Ever since Malcolm Gladwell wrote *The Tipping Point*,[14] business authors have written books laden with stories, much more so than was done in the past. This development has given business storytellers a treasure trove of stories to tell.

Imagine sitting down with your CEO to discuss the many strategic choices she might pursue and you want to introduce the idea of a keystone habit—one that would have a flow-on effect on many other behaviours in the business. You might tell this story about Alcoa.

Back in 1987 Alcoa appointed a new CEO, Paul O'Neill, an unusual choice because he came from the public sector. Because investors had begun to grumble about Alcoa's recent financial performance, one of O'Neill's first duties was to brief a group of Wall Street analysts on where he planned to take the company. Addressing the analysts in the ballroom of a New York hotel, the new CEO surprised them by forgoing the normal reassuring pitch, instead telling them he was going to focus on safety. At that point there was at least one accident every week at Alcoa, some of them fatal. O'Neill announced he would aim for zero accidents. When the confused analysts tried to ask about profit projections, taxes, controlling costs and the like, O'Neill steered them back towards his focus on safety. He even gave the audience a safety briefing, pointing out the ballroom's exits. The analysts all thought O'Neill was mad, and they raced back to their offices determined to recommend to their clients that they sell their stock in Alcoa.

It would turn out to be the worst financial advice those analysts ever gave. A year later, Alcoa's profits would hit a record high. Thirteen years later, on O'Neill's retirement, the firm's annual net income would be five times greater than it had been when the CEO was hired. His company would also be one of the safest in the world—in some plants, several years went by without a single serious accident. Alcoa's focus on a single important habit—a keystone habit—had prompted many other benefits to flow throughout the organisation, including financial success.

I read this story in Charles Duhigg's fabulous *The Power of Habit*.[15] His telling of the story is elaborate, taking up three pages of the book. For the purposes of oral storytelling, however, you would shorten it and strip out much of the detail. You would concentrate on making it evocative enough that your listener could see it happening while at the same time ensuring you make your business point.

Scientific Experiments

One of my favourite types of stories to tell is the scientific experiment because I get to make a business point backed by peer-reviewed research. Experiments are often told as stories; in fact, Robert Cialdini has noted that some of the most compelling science articles are written as mystery stories.[16] Business books often recount these stories, which makes finding them quite easy. An important thing to remember when recounting an experiment is to mention the institution involved, especially if it's a prestigious university. As I explain when I talk about story sources in *Putting Stories to Work: Mastering Business Storytelling* Chapter 5, this detail can increase the influence of the story.

One great story involves an experiment done by social psychologist Edward Deci at the University of Rochester in the 1970s. University students were asked to work on a simple spatial puzzle. Half of the participants were paid to do this task and the others were not. After a student had worked on the puzzle for a while, a researcher entered the room, asked the subject to wait while they set up the next phase of the experiment, and then left. It was now that the experiment really started. A video camera recorded what happened after the researcher exited the room. The people who were being paid to do the task stopped working on the puzzle and just waited. Those who weren't being paid continued to work. The experiment clearly showed that explicit rewards can undermine intrinsic motivation.[17]

Movies and Broadcasts

'What have the Romans ever done for us?' Remember this classic line from the Monty Python movie *The Life of Brian*? The members of the People's Front of Judea are huddled around a table in a small, dark room, complaining about the Romans. When their leader, Reg, asks what the Romans have ever given them, one of the underlings pipes up: 'The aqueduct'. 'Oh yeah, yeah they gave us that. That's true', says Reg. Another person then says, 'And the sanitation', which prompts a chorus of voices: 'Irrigation... medicine... education... health... And the wine...' Reg, of course, refuses to concede the point.

Well-known scenes in movies can make excellent work analogies as they are mini stories. You might quote Reg after saying something like: 'All this complaining about IT reminds me of that scene in the movie *Life of Brian*'. Of course, you need to pick a movie that will resonate with your audience.

The Tom Hanks movie *Apollo 13* has a great scene where there is an emergency in the space capsule and the crew needs to be told how to build a new carbon dioxide filter using a limited set of equipment. It's up to the technicians back on Earth to work it out or the astronauts will die. Under extreme time pressure, the technicians start throwing parts across a table, desperately looking for an answer. Just before it's too late, they figure out a solution and the astronauts are saved.

This scene makes for a convincing story about innovation, how constraints such as limited parts or resources can be a condition for creativity. It's also inspirational. I can imagine telling this story to rally a team facing a crazy deadline that they haven't been properly resourced to meet.

Even advertisements can offer good stories. My sister, Stacey, is the principal of a New South Wales high school with the largest number of Indigenous students in Australia. She recently gathered together 60 people—students, teachers, parents, community leaders—to help her formulate the school's strategy. Before they got going, Stacey wanted to set the tone for the workshop and also reinforce a basic principle of her school: Our students have the whole world open to them and we must never squash their dreams. So to start the session, Stacey showed the attendees a commercial for the activewear company Under Armor featuring the story of Misty Copeland. When Copeland was young, the African American dancer was told she would never make it because her body shape was all wrong. Now she's a principal dancer for the American Ballet Theatre.

Copeland 's story grounded the strategy session. Everyone understood that they needed to create an environment where the students could shine, regardless of their current capabilities and backgrounds.

Now this book is all about oral storytelling: no props, no costumes, no stage directions, just true stories. That last phrase happens to be the tagline of a great storytelling podcast called *The Moth*. It started as a New York story competition—a story slam—where people from all walks of life got up on stage and told a real-life story in five minutes, without notes. The best story of the night won. Today, *The Moth* runs similar events all over the United States and the regular podcast features the very best stories. Listening to these broadcasts helps you pinpoint what makes a good story. Just like good writers are good readers, good storytellers are good story listeners.

Another great story-based podcast is *This American Life*, hosted by Ira Glass. Each week I tune in to hear beautifully told stories of real-life happenings accompanied by well-chosen soundtracks and interviews with the various protagonists.

Here are some of my other storytelling podcast favourites, which I suggest you add to your playlist:

- *StartUp*
- *Serial*
- *Mystery Show*
- *Freakonomics Radio.*

Your Story Discovery Journal

So now you know that there are plenty of places where you can find stories. And you know that you need to go out and get good stories rather than just wait for them to land in your lap. You should also understand that the difference between storytelling in general and business storytelling is that the latter is systematic and purposeful, and that a useful tool to accomplish this is a story discovery journal. Journalling can be done at the end of the day, say before you go to bed, or on the fly as you discover stories.

Many businesspeople think that little happens to them that's story-worthy, but nothing could be further from the truth. You just need some questions to prompt you and a few minutes of quiet time to reflect on your day. I find that these three questions are a good place to start:

- What stood out for me today?
- Did I hear any good stories?
- Did I read any good stories?

You can expect these questions to generate a few potential stories. For each one, ask yourself this question:

- What's the point this story makes?

If the story would help you to make a business point, then it's worth trying out. If it works in practice, then add it to your repertoire.

You can go old-school and use a paper notebook, or you can simply open a Word document and keep appending entries. My preference is to use the iPhone app Evernote and keep all my stories in one Evernote notebook. Whichever approach you choose, it's important to keep all your entries together for quick reference. Things change at work all the time: potential stories you passed over in the past can quickly become relevant in the future.

Story journalling only needs to be done in short blocks, say five minutes—don't forget to allow some time to appreciate the stories you've discovered. For this to become a habit, set a time to do it that triggers the behaviour, such as finishing dinner or having a nightcap. To begin with, set yourself the small goal of doing it every day for a week, then build from there. Within a month, you could have 60 stories ready to tell.

* * *

Story discovery is the foundation of business storytelling. By developing a keen eye that can discern stories from story imposters, and the ability to notice the many stories that constantly swirl around you, you will put yourself in the best possible position to find and tell stories that engage, influence and inspire. With your stories in hand, you then need to learn how to remember them so they can be told off the cuff.

ABOUT THE AUTHOR

Shawn Callahan is a sought-after keynote speaker, international business consultant and executive coach who works with global organisations such as Mars, Danone, Allianz, SAP, Tesco and Shell. He is the founder of Anecdote, the world 's largest business storytelling company. Anecdote helps leaders and sellers around the world to find and tell oral stories with impact. Its programs are delivered in ten languages in 24 countries, and counting.

Shawn's book *Putting Stories to Work: Mastering Business Storytelling* is the most practical guide available to developing your skills as a business storyteller. It won a gold medal in the 2017 Axiom Business Book Awards.

Shawn holds a bachelor's degree with honours in geography and archaeology from the Australian National University. He is married, with two grown-up daughters, and lives in Melbourne, Australia. He can be found at www.anecdote.com.

BIBLIOGRAPHY

1. Wheatley, M.J. (2003). 'Leadership and the Power of Chaos.' Presentation at Leadership & Learning: A Design Media Discussion Forum. San Francisco, 27 June.

2. Aēsop (2015). 'The Aēsop Story.' aesop.com/au/article/who-weare.html

3. *This American Life (2013). 'No Coincidence, No Story!' 1 March, Episode 489.*

4. Shettleworth, S.T. (1998). *Cognition, Evolution and Behavior.* New York, Oxford University Press.

5. Newsome, M. (2007). 'He Took on the Whole Power-tool Industry.' Inc., 24 January. inc.com/magazine/20050701/disruptor-gass.html

6. Roth, D.L. (1998). *Crazy from the Heat.* New York, Hyperion.

7. Orr, J.E. (1996). *Talking about Machines: An Ethnography of a Modern Job.* Ithaca, NY, Cornell University Press.

8. Pratchett, T. (1992). *Witches Abroad.* London, Corgi Books, p. 8.

9. Rayton, B. and T. Dodge (2012). 'The Evidence: Employee Engagement Task Force "Nailing the Evidence" Workgroup.' London, Engage for Success.

10. Peters, T.J. and R.H. Waterman (1982). *In Search of Excellence: Lessons from America's Best-run Companies.* New York, Harper & Row, p. 192.

11. Forbes (2015). 'America's Largest Private Companies.' forbes.com/companies/mars

12. Vogt, E.E., J. Brown and D. Isaacs (2003). *The Art of Powerful Questions: Catalyzing Insight, Innovation, and Action.* Mill Valley, CA, Whole Systems Associates.

13. Schenk, M. and S. Callahan (2015). *Character Trumps Credentials: 170 Questions that Help Leaders Find and Tell Great Stories* (eBook). Pascoe Vale Sth, Vic., Pepperberg Press. anecdote.com/wp-content/

14. Gladwell, M. (2000). *The Tipping Point: How Little Things Can Make a Big Difference.* Boston, Little, Brown and Company.

15. Duhigg, C. (2012). *The Power of Habit: Why We Do What We Do and How to Change.* London, William Heinemann.

16. Cialdini, R.B. (2005). 'What's the Best Secret Device for Engaging Student Interest? The Answer Is in the Title.' *Journal of Social and Clinical Psychology,* 24(1): 22–9.

17. Kohn, A. (1993). *Punished by Rewards: The Trouble with Gold Stars, Incentive Plans, A's, Praise, and Other Bribes.* Boston, Houghton Mifflin, pp. 69–70

Inside your heart is a tiny place where all knowledge and wisdom resides.

~ **Hopi Proverb**

CREATIVITY AND INNOVATION

ABOUT THE CHAPTER

We seem to have spent so much time in the last 100+ years trying to drive efficiency and effectiveness into our processes, in-deed, those are often two of the main drivers of KM implementations. How to do things faster, with more quality, with better outcomes, reduce waste, reduce re-work. These are not bad things, but in our push to be effective and efficient many of our organizations have removed time for reflection, for questioning, for considering alternatives from the process.

Innovation and creativity are powerful skills that we need for differentiation purposes in our organizations, and to which we are attracted as humans. Sadly, too often we let self-criticism and anxiety as well as the drive for efficiency and effectiveness hold us back from being creative.

In the right environment, and with the right tools and techniques, we can progress past these blocks and let creativity and innovation become a regular, useful part of our daily lives, careers, and workplaces. This chapter outlines how to incorporate creativity and innovation into your knowledge management activities and why it is important that you do so.

Please cite as:

Barnes, S. (2018). Creativity and innovation. In J. P. Girard & J. L. Girard (Eds.), *Knowledge management matters: Words of wisdom from leading practitioners* (73-89). Macon, GA: Sagology.

4

CREATIVITY AND INNOVATION

BY STEPHANIE BARNES

Introduction

To be creative, you don't need to be an artist, creativity isn't about painting, drawing, or art at all, those outcomes are just one manifestation of creativity. Creativity is about doing things differently, looking for alternatives, keeping an open mind, asking questions, having new experiences, and continuing to learn, as well as being able to use seemingly unrelated concepts to solve a problem or answer a question. We all have the ability to create new ideas, make new decisions, do something new, have a different outcome. In our jobs we can introduce creativity in small ways, just asking questions or challenging assumptions in a meeting, or sitting down with someone new at lunch and learning about who they are and about their experiences.

Knowledge management, critical thinking, creativity, and innovation would seem to be different ideas and disciplines, but in fact they can and do enable and enrich each other as in the process of addressing the question: what if that's not true? This chapter will illuminate how knowledge management, critical thinking, creativity, intersect with innovation to challenge assumptions and find novel solutions to questions and problems.

This chapter outlines how to create space for knowledge creation and how this leads to innovation. We also take a look at the different ways of incorporating creativity into the organization and the knowledge management strategy so that creativity, innovation, and knowledge management align to support the organization's goals and objectives as recommended in the book the author co-authored on how to design a successful KM strategy (Barnes, 2015).

Definitions

Ba, Nonaka discusses the idea of "ba" in his book, "The Knowledge Creating Company," as well as other published articles; "ba" is the idea of making space for (knowledge) creation (Nonaka, 1995). This idea of space is through the use of physical and/or virtual space, and includes the idea of (emergent) relationships and mental/intellectual/emotional space (reflection, and just being).

Creativity is defined as: the ability to transcend traditional ideas, rules, patterns, relationships, or the like, and to create meaningful new ideas, forms, methods, interpretations, etc.; originality, progressiveness, or imagination: the need for creativity in modern industry; creativity in the performing arts. Another definition says that creativity is the reorganization of experience into new configurations: a function of knowledge, imagination, and evaluation (Dictionary.com, 2015).

Critical thinking is the objective analysis and evaluation of an issue in order to form a judgment.

Design thinking is characterized by being purposive; human centered; a balance of analytical and creative; uses abductive reasoning, i.e. inference from best available explanation; and iterative, it uses prototyping and play testing to achieve success.

Innovation is defined as: a new idea, more effective device or process, it can be viewed as the application of better solutions that meet new requirements, unarticulated needs, or existing market needs. The term innovation can be defined as something original and more effective and, as a consequence, new, that "breaks into" the market or society (Wikipedia (1), 2015).

Knowledge management is defined as: the process of capturing, developing, sharing, and effectively using organizational knowledge. It refers to a multi-disciplinary approach to achieving organizational objectives by making the best use of knowledge (Wikipedia, (2), 2015).

Companies that have Embraced Creativity

The following are examples of three organizations that have used some form of creativity to enhance their innovation and other operational activities.

Xerox

The Xerox PARC Artist-in-Residence program ran during the 1990's at Xerox PARC in California. The program invited artists who use new media into PARC and paired them with scientists who often were researching the same media. The artists were expected to revitalize the research bringing new ideas and perspectives. The cross fertilization was also expected to deliver interesting art and new scientific innovations. The program was originally planned as a one-year experiment, but it was so successful it actually ran for six years from 1993-1999.

PAIR also helped PARC keep the research relevant to the company. In fact, what artists fundamentally make are documents, particularly new forms and genres of them. Artists discover new kinds of documents, new uses for the documents, and Xerox is after all The Document Company. The process and the technology to express or create these are tightly intertwined. They probably best develop simultaneously and what better way to do this than to partner artists and scientists (Harris, 1999).

Equiva Services

Equiva Services is the support services company for joint venture companies formed by Shell Oil Company, Texaco, and Saudi Refining (an affiliate of Saudi Aramco). Equiva Services provides services such as learning and development, human resources, information technology, and marketing. The joint venture companies were facing severe pressures to enter new markets with innovative products and delivery systems pertaining to downstream oil. Participants in a learning lab went out on field trips to study "new economy" companies to learn how they leverage creativity and high performance. Once they completed their information gathering, their next challenge was to synthesize their findings and make sense of it all.

Artist Todd Siler guided the group in making five-dimensional prototypes (sculptures) using his five-dimensional (5-d) model-building process that incorporates (1d) words, (2d) images, (3d) structures, (4d) motions, and (5d) symbols. This process enabled participants to give form to their ideas and make unconscious (tacit) ideas conscious (explicit). Their artwork sparked inquiry, dialogue, storytelling, and reflection among the group. According to Nick Nissley and Gary Jusela, researchers involved in this project, these sculptures were the structural capital that "led to the telling of stories about how the energy of imagination and knowledge from the participants' field visits could be harnessed into intellectual capital."

Using art to visualize information and ideas is a simple and powerful way to make knowledge explicit. The art process made visible what it takes to operate in the new economy. According to Siler: "Using a wide range of disciplines in the arts, from sculpting, drawing, music, and literature to electronic arts, can really help people see their problems and opportunities differently. Art-making also helps people tap into their human potential, which every organization is founded on." He points out that if people talk about their ideas without visualizing them, it is easy to misinterpret what people mean: "You can have the best technology and the best position within a market, but if that human communication piece doesn't work it impacts on everything from the shareholders to the customers to the services rendered and delivered."[1] (VanGundy, 2005).

LexisNexis

"My own special area of focus is the performing arts and their applicability to corporate training and development. Teaching the soft skills by means of procedures 'bulletized' on PowerPoint charts can provide a framework, but the real challenge of utilizing those skills is to know how to fill in the spaces between the bullets or to know how to shift to another framework when the real world doesn't cooperate with bulleted procedures. Actors, especially improvisational actors, have been training their minds for centuries to deal with the unanticipated or, rather, to 'anticipate surprise.' All of the learnings of improvisational acting apply to learning soft skills in the workplace.

"At LexisNexis, it's very common for me to facilitate the work of a group of people who haven't worked together before and who often aren't located in the same city, country, or hemisphere. Their challenge can be equated to that of an improv team: To jointly create a coherent narrative from little more than, 'Here's the goal. Figure out how to get there.' Team members have to take that input and create [metaphorically] a long-form improv performance out of it, using the skills of the improvisational performer. They have to decide what their roles on the team are going to be. They have to really learn about true collaboration, which requires becoming comfortable with trusting one's instincts, with flexing one's reaction to follow the shift in the narrative, with supporting others and trusting them to support you. And all of their actions must be geared toward advancing the team toward a goal or, in improv terms, 'telling the story.' Team members must identify promising directions to follow, accept offers for exploration, relate all the various stimuli to the emerging narrative, strike out into risky areas, relinquish trying to control the ultimate outcome, and ultimately create a coherent result that incorporates as many of the threads as possible. In the best improv and the best business teams, there are no stars, no upstaging. The team is the star." (VanGundy, 2005).

These examples are meant to illustrate the variety of ways that creativity can be used within an organization to enhance, not only innovation, as the Xerox example shows, but to improve collaboration and communication as well as employee performance. With these examples in mind the next sections consider various means and models for integrating creativity and innovation into an organization's knowledge management and other operational activities.

---

[1] Researchers Nick Nissley and Gary Jusela's study on Equiva was published in 2002 by ASTD.

Critical Thinking and Knowledge Management

Critical thinking underlies all of knowledge management; it is what pushes us to learn, and learning is at the heart of knowledge management. Curiosity drives both critical thinking and learning. Having the curiosity to ask "why" five times will help us get to the root of a problem or understand our assumptions when we ask the question "what if that's not true?". Asking questions can help us see things differently, by helping us to see things from a different perspective. Without the ability to think/reflect and to question our experiences, the whole foundation of knowledge management crumbles.

Critical thinking encourages us to keep an open mind and gather information and evidence before coming to a conclusion.

As we know, knowledge management is the set of processes and tools that underlies any knowledge-based activity. The reality of the world we live in is that everything is knowledge-based and there is something to be learned from every success and failure. The question is how to facilitate, enhance, and improve efficiency, effectiveness, and risk informed decision making of any process/activity through the use of knowledge management activities?

Improved efficiency and effectiveness and risk informed decision making comes from finding new, creative, innovative solutions and thinking critically about the current situation and assumptions. How do we do this? We do things like:

1. Ask, "what if that's not true?"
2. Ask "five whys"
3. Think inside the box (apply scarcity/constraints)
4. Reflect
5. Understand your own story/motivation, what assumptions are you making?
6. Change the rules
7. Be curious
8. Independent thinking/diversity
9. Sharpen your senses (listen/mindfulness, appreciate beauty)
10. Embrace uncertainty
11. Balance logic and imagination
12. Balance body and mind
13. Make new connections

Additionally, using knowledge management activities can aid in this process. KM activities such as:

1. Business driven action learning (learning through doing)
2. Coaching and mentoring

3. Communities of practice

4. External assessment and benchmarking

5. Knowledge capture from projects

6. Knowledge exchange

7. Knowledge harvesting from individuals

8. Lessons learned

9. Peer assists

10. Project learning

11. Organizational Learning, Training

Why are these knowledge management activities the ones that support innovation? Because they bring people together who are not normally together, they provide space for asking questions and learning from each other. These activities provide processes and tools to facilitate the discovery of new solutions and creation of new knowledge.

Thinking about this a little differently, we can use creativity and innovation to enhance knowledge management; we do this by applying critical thinking to our knowledge management activities (Mackey, 2016). For example, instead of just looking at other similar projects that have been done within our organization or industry and learning from them, we can think critically about other industries that might have had a similar strategic issue and how they solved it. A nuclear power plant may learn how to resolve a training issue from the automotive industry or from an NGO that had also struggled with just-in-time training delivery. Alternatively, what results have we discovered by participating in a Community of Practice, in a Peer Assist, or After Action Review and how does this impact what we already thought we knew?

At this point, we need to consider what is meant by organized versus unorganized knowledge. Organized knowledge includes things that have been documented, in books, journals, repositories, libraries, databases, and slide decks, that we know/have access to. Whereas unorganized knowledge is knowledge that hasn't been discovered or formalized yet either because the experiments haven't been performed or it resides in the heads of people we haven't met yet.

What allows us to pass back and forth between organized and unorganized is the use of critical thinking. Critical thinking allows us to question what we know and to ask questions to discover new knowledge, but it also allows us to take the new knowledge and organize it into new or existing models. Critical thinking allows us to apply "the rules" but it also allows us to question and break "the rules" in order to make new discoveries and learn: this is creativity and innovation in action.

Design Thinking as a Component of Knowledge Management

Another way of incorporating creativity and innovation into knowledge management is through the use of design thinking. There are five design principles: purposive, human centered, balance of analytical and creative, abductive reasoning, and iterative. They are applied to knowledge management in the following ways.

Purposive: we look at the organization's strategy, goals, and objectives and assess how knowledge management best supports those activities. The knowledge management strategy outlines how the organization's goals and objectives are furthered through the application of knowledge management activities.

Human centered: the best knowledge management implementations consider the people of the organization, e.g. how they work, what makes their work-lives easier, what the culture of the organization is like and works with those requirements to make the organization more efficient and effective in its knowledge processes and activities.

A balance of analytical and creative: KM should be a balance of analytical and creative. It should capture knowledge and make it reusable, but it also needs to leave space, ba, to allow for knowledge creation. This space can look like lots of different things, e.g. giving employees 10% of their time for projects they want to work on/explore, foosball tables, basketball courts, gyms, art/creativity space, and communities of interest; activities that encourage different connections to be made.

Abductive reasoning: this sums up the belief in KM in general. It can be very difficult to prove a causal link between improved knowledge activities and improved organizational performance, metrics and ROI continue to be a significant hurdle for many organizations. However, anyone who has experience with implementing knowledge management successfully knows that efficiency and effectiveness in an organization are improved through the use of knowledge management activities.

Iterative: successful KM starts small and grows. It starts with an over-all strategy and plan, but then moves to pilots, which bring in small parts of the organization, so that lessons can be learned and adjustments made as the people, process, and supporting technology are implemented across the organization.

An example of design thinking in the application of knowledge management, comes from work the author did early in her knowledge management career. The organization she worked with (a business unit in a large high technology firm) had failed in at least two earlier attempts to roll-out a knowledge management technology platform that was primarily to be used for collaboration and sharing documentation. The author took the approach of asking the users how they wanted to use the system, what would help them and make their jobs easier. She also took a phased, iterative approach, so that each team/group/department received individual attention. This had not been done before, and although it took several years to get 7000+ users using the system, the roll-out was a huge success and people loved and valued the technology and how it supported them in their jobs.

Connection Between Knowledge Management and Creativity

As previously highlighted knowledge management is the set of tools that underlies any knowledge-based activity; and everything is knowledge-based. The question is how to facilitate, enhance, and improve efficiency and effectiveness of any process/activity through the use of knowledge management activities. Improved efficiency and effectiveness comes from finding new, creative, innovative solutions. How do we find these new, creative, innovative solutions?

Two books can give us insights on solving this problem. The first is in the process of being written, the other was published in 2000. The book that is in the process of being written is by Ger Driesen and is about what we can learn about learning from Vincent Van Gogh; the second was written by Michael J. Gelb and is entitled, "How to Think Like Leonardo da Vinci: Seven Steps to Genius Every Day."

From Van Gogh we learn:

1. Think inside the box (apply scarcity/constraints)
2. Practice/study
3. Reflect
4. Understand your own story/motivation
5. When you master a level change the rules
6. Value solitude, not loneliness
7. Circumstances: join them or beat them

From Leonardo da Vinci we learn:

1. Curiosity
2. Independent thinking/diversity
3. Sharpen your senses (listen/mindfulness, appreciate beauty)
4. Embrace uncertainty
5. Balance logic and imagination
6. Balance body and mind
7. Make new connections

To do these things we need to have the space, or as Nonaka identified, the ba for knowledge creation.

Using these constructs gleaned from artists, as well as specific knowledge management activities to aid in innovation helps us to discover new ways of doing things.

How a Creative Mindset can be Adopted in our Organizations

A creative mindset is comprised of the items that we can learn from da Vinci or Van Gogh as described earlier in this chapter, as well as the practice of innumerable other artists. All of these items have been summarized and put into a framework developed by Age of Artists, a consultancy, education provider, and research institute based in Germany.

Their framework, pictured elsewhere in this section, works from the outside in towards the middle, using artistic practices and attitudes to transform traditional responses. In the model, the organizational situation appears on the left-hand side, while the artistic practices and attitudes are on the right. Transformational activities, such as leadership, consulting, education, coaching, and cooperation connect the two sides and allow the artistic activities to act upon the situations on the left side.

Circumstances, like dealing with a market, that are complex, changing quickly, uncertain, or volatile are all considered. The traditional response in these situations might be to try to simplify things, in the case of complexity; slow them down, in the case of acceleration; control them, when they are uncertain; or approach them with resistance in the case of volatility. However, by using artistic practices and attitudes in a transformational approach we can move our organizations to an alternative response which will provide a more balanced, engaged result. We will have diversity instead of simplicity; a sense of purpose instead of deceleration; autonomy in the place of control; and elasticity rather than numerous rules and exceptions, in the case of volatility.

In adapting a creative mindset, and applying artistic practices to an organizational situation, we start by identifying the business problem we are trying to solve, then we decide which practice we want to start with: perceiving, reflecting, creating, or performing. We can start with any of the activities and move through the others as part of the process of arriving at the response/resolution of the problem.

In arriving at a resolution, we are best served if we adopt artistic attitudes, like curiosity (like asking why five times, or challenging assumptions), being passionate about what we are working on, being confident that there is a solution, and being resilient enough to bounce back when we experience failures or set-backs. It is the persistence that develops through these activities that is the key to finding a solution.

It is in this transformational phase that knowledge management activities, like peer assists or communities of practice, to name two, can help. Also, the critical thinking that underlies so much of knowledge management is important here. The awareness of the need to ask questions, challenge assumptions, and look at things differently is one of the reasons why bringing people in from outside can be really helpful, and it is one of the reasons why artist-in-residence programs have been successful.

Artists look at things differently, they have different backgrounds and different expectations than most of the people typically hired into our organizations. As discussed in the examples at the beginning of the chapter, Xerox ran an artist-in-residence program for six years (five years longer than planned) due to the success of matching artists with the scientists in their research and development facility and the innovations that resulted from this matching.

Age of Artists works with organizations to facilitate solutions that are not possible using existing thinking. As an example, an SVP (Senior Vice Presidnet) of Procurement in an organization that Age of Artists members worked with wanted to identify the root causes of process inefficiencies and opportunities in order to create a harmonious work experience for procurement operations employees. Age of Artists used their framework to complete ethnographic on-site research. The research identified five key issues that were affecting the productivity and satisfaction of staff both inside the procurement team and elsewhere in the organization. The team then worked closely with the executive team to create empathy for the day to day challenges that were impeding business progress and this in turn led to 35 actionable recommendations for the organization.

Another example of a project completed using the sensibilities of artists applied to an organizational problem is the case of an internal department responsible for processes and applications. The organization already had a team of designers in place but was still challenged by low adoption of their solutions. It was difficult for the internal designers to convince senior stakeholders and internal clients to recognize the criticality of this problem. A pilot ethnographic study was conducted which revealed significant hidden issues that were not discovered through the traditional requirements and design process. A decision was made to embed user researchers into the individual departments within the organization. Through examples and early results all members of the organization understood the value of user research and the positive impact it brings to tackling complex tasks. The team developed and rolled out an integrated approach bringing together business, technology, design and research skills to work together collaboratively with improved means of understanding.

Challenges & Opportunities	Traditional Response (Confused with intended result)	Suggested Alternate Response (Creativity Culture)	Transformation Activities	Artistic Attitude	Artistic Practice
Complexity	Simplicity	Diversity		Curiosity	Perceive
Acceleration	Deceleration	Purpose	Leadership, Consulting, Education, Coaching, Cooperation	Passion	Reflect
Uncertainty	Control	Autonomy		Confidence	Play
Volatility	Resistance	Elasticity		Resilience	Perform

Figure 4-1. Age of Artists Framework, adapted from and used with permission of www.ageofartists.org

Tools for Developing Creativity

Since creativity is about looking at the world differently and asking different questions, how can we develop it? The chapter has outlined some models and methodologies, as well as some knowledge management activities and these all help and give some organizationally-focused activities, but what about on an individual level? After-all organizations are made up of people, how can they become more creative so that they can use these organizational tools even more successfully?

On an individual level people need to be encouraged to get enough sleep. Having enough rest is key to being creative. If we are tired and sleep deprived, we're not going to think about asking questions and looking at things differently, we're going to do things quickly and easily: the same way they have always been done. So getting enough sleep is critical to being creative. Other activities that help develop creativity include playing, exercising, going to the theatre or a concert, learning a language or a musical instrument, reading a book, going for a walk in nature, day dreaming, meditating, learning something new. What do all of these have in common? They take us out of our routines, expose us to something new or different, they give us space to look at the world differently. They encourage us to ask questions and experiment, which develops and expands our creativity.

For example, if you were to try painting or drawing, you might try out new ways of making a mark on a canvas using different tools and mediums. Some of these methods and mediums you might like, some you might not like, but the experimentation is key. Learning that even if you don't like it at a certain stage there is something to be learned from that, and to be built upon for future stages and experiments. This encouragement to experiment in one area of life can lead to looking at things differently in other areas of life.

Another example is exercising, taking a walk in nature, or meditating. Not only are these activities good for our health and stress levels, but they take us out of our heads and into our bodies, helping us to take a break, giving our brains a rest and giving us some space to let other questions and ideas come into our heads rather than the ones we have been sitting staring at all day/week/month. Creativity needs space.

Why Worry About Creativity and Innovation?

Encouraging creativity has several benefits, they fall into two main categories: employee engagement/satisfaction and competitive advantage.

On a personal level introducing creativity directly impacts the employee. It increases their motivation, deep concentration, and most importantly engagement. Creativity also improves relationships, because of the communication aspect of asking and learning that happens through undertaking a creative endeavour. It allows people to develop their talents, as well as improve their resilience and adaptability, meaning that their ability to cope with uncertainty and change is improved.

The organization, Creative Huddle (2015), conducted an ethnographic survey on creativity in the workplace and found that it makes people feel: empowered, motivated, inspired, engaged, energized, and proud. In this same study respondents reported that they believed creativity had impact on:

1. Motivation 97%
2. Engagement 91%
3. Productivity 89%
4. Happiness 88%
5. Profits 71%
6. Worklife balance 64%

These findings highlight the importance of creativity in the workplace, illustrating that creativity doesn't just have a personal impact but also an organizational impact. Which leads us to the competitive advantage of creativity.

With today's pace of change it is imperative to constantly improve and innovate in order to stay ahead of the competition. And, in-deed, we seem to have spent a great deal of time in the last 100+ years trying to drive efficiency and effectiveness into our processes in order to stay ahead of the competition (those are often two of the main drivers of KM implementations). How to do things faster, with more quality, with better outcomes, reduce waste, reduce re-work. These are not bad things, but in our push to be effective and efficient many of our organizations have removed time for reflection, for questioning, for considering alternatives out of the process. Re-introducing time through the use of creativity helps to reverse some of what was lost through our excessive focus on efficiency and effectiveness and allows our organizations to remain competitive.

Knowledge Management supported by critical thinking, creativity, and innovation can help reintroduce some space to think and create. Enabling this aspect of Knowledge Management supports looking at the problem/challenge differently and encourages using solutions that may have been developed in other organizations/ industries (Evans, 2013).

The use of creativity and reintroduction of space/ba can result in objectives being achieved more readily because staff are thinking about what they are doing, and not just racing blindly towards a finish line.

Conclusion

Rather than getting caught up in the routine processes of knowledge management, we can enhance and improve knowledge management with critical thinking and creativity to find innovative solutions to efficiency and effectiveness, competitive advantage as well as in risk informed decision making. The knowledge management program still aligns with the organization's vision, objectives, and needs, as explained in Barnes (2015), but it incorporates a new component: creativity, to enhance innovation, which allows the organization and its staff to continue evolving, developing, learning, and maturing.

ABOUT THE AUTHOR

Stephanie Barnes is an artist and knowledge management consultant, she has a Bachelor of Business Administration in accounting and an Master of Business Administration in information technology. She works with organizations to make better use of what they know, utilizing her strategic business knowledge, critical thinking, and creativity in the process.

Stephanie is also a member of Age of Artists www.ageofartists.org, a consultancy, education provider, and research institute that focuses on identifying and transferring the creative practices and problem-framing patterns of art into other disciplines and contexts in order to empower individuals, teams and organizations to resolve complex and systemic business challenges as well as promoting individual growth and skill development for all.

Where to find Stephanie:

Missing Puzzle Piece Consulting missingpuzzlepiececonsulting.com
Stephanie Barnes Art
Art of Innovation http://www.artofinnovation.net/
Age of Artists http://www.ageofartists.org/about-us/our-core-team/
Twitter @MPuzzlePiece
SlideShare http://www.slideshare.net/stephaniebarnes/
LinkedIn https://www.linkedin.com/in/stephanieabarnes/
Instagram https://www.instagram.com/mppc1967/
Xing: https://www.xing.com/profile/Stephanie_Barnes3

BIBLIOGRAPHY

Barnes, Stephanie and Nick Milton. (2015). *Designing a Successful KM Strategy: A Guide for the Knowledge Management Professional.* Medford: Information Today, Inc.

Creative Huddle. (2016). *"Creativity impacts engagement, motivation, productivity and more!"*, Retrieved from http://www.creativehuddle.co.uk/creativity-impacts-engagement-motivation-productivity-and-more on October 24, 2017 at 3:51pm CET.

Dictionary.com (2015) *Definition of Creativity*, Retrieved from http://dictionary.reference.com/browse/creativity, accessed on Dec 4, 2015 at 3:55pm CET.

Evans, Hugh. (2013). *Creativity is the Next Competitive Advantage*, Retrieved from http://enterprisearchitects.com/creativity-is-the-next-competitive-advantage/, on January 20, 2016 at 12:11pm CET.

Harris, Craig (editor). (1999). *Art and Innovation: The Xerox PARC Artist-in-Residence Program.* Cambridge, Massachusetts: MIT Press.

Mackey, Susan and Rose Ann Schwartz. (2016). *Developing Critical Thinking Through the Arts.* Retrieved from http://www.visionsonlearningdifferences.com/main3.html, on January 20, 2016 at 12:09pm CET.

Nonaka, Ikujiro and Hirotaka Takeuchi. (1995). *The Knowledge Creating Company: How Japanese Companies Create the Dynamics of Innovation.* New York: Oxford University Press.

VanGundy, Arthur B. and Linda Naiman. (2005). *Orchestrating Collaboration at Work: Using music, improv, storytelling, and other arts to improve teamwork.* United States of America: John Wiley & Sons.

Wikipedia (1). (2015). Definition of Innovation, Retrieved from https://en.wikipedia.org/wiki/Innovation, on Dec 4, 2015 at 4:12pm.

Wikipedia (2). (2015). Definition of Knowledge Management, Retrieved from https://en.wikipedia.org/wiki/Knowledge_management#cite_note-2UNC-2, on Dec 4, 2015 at 4:07pm CET.

Knowledge is rooted in all things — the world is a library.

~ **Lakota Proverb**

WHEN THEY LEAVE THEIR KNOWLEDGE (AND NETWORKS) LEAVE WITH THEM

ABOUT THE CHAPTER

As I was growing up and entering the workplace it was common for new joiners to have a probationary or apprenticeship period where you learned from watching then doing under supervision.

Depending on the profession that apprenticeship period could be anything from 6 months to a year and at the end rather like a pilot you were deemed competent to fly solo.

The assumption was that you were likely to be with that organization for a long period and that when you eventually did leave (or retire) your knowledge would have been passed on to those who would replace you.

Today employees are much more transient in nature and few organizations run apprenticeship programs: the c.v. is not about who you worked for, it is more about what you worked on (and achieved). It is highly likely that during their working life someone in their 20's today will have worked for more than 5 employers (if not going solo as part of the 'gig' economy).

Organizations have to plan for this increasing turnover and changing demographics. Their systems have to cater for a transient workforce.

This chapter is in three parts: The Challenge; The Tools; and The Future. It examines ways to address the risk of knowledge loss; in one case it looks at the issue thru the lens of a Chinese PhD Student Jonny Jiang who I mentored while we were engaged in helping to establish a UK Charity.

This chapter is:

Please cite as:

Corney, P.J. (2018). When they leave their knowledge (and networks) leave with them. In J. P. Girard & J. L. Girard (Eds.), *Knowledge management matters: Words of wisdom from leading practitioners* (91-111). Macon, GA: Sagology.

5

WHEN THEY LEAVE THEIR KNOWLEDGE (AND NETWORKS) LEAVE WITH THEM

BY PAUL J. CORNEY

Part 1 - The Challenge

How To Conduct Knowledge Capture in a Hurry

It's August in the Middle East where the temperature rarely dips below 30c at night and reaches 50c+ during the day. Contrast that with winter where snow is on mountains that trap carbon emissions severely impacting air quality.

I've been there 7 times in the past 12 months and seen all the seasons and how they impact people's demeanours. How festivals such as Ramadan affects productivity (while enriching the soul of those who follow its strictures), how the New Year which occurs in the spring makes people look longingly towards the future and how April seems to be everyone's favourite month: clear blue skies, snow-capped mountains, a purity about the air and a profusion of flowers.

July and August are the hot months when recruitment people at universities globally are most busy and when many organizations in the Middle East and Asia see their talent take sabbaticals to go back to school to further career prospects.

I am with a client where 3 of the most talented minds who have been the core team on a project have been offered the chance to further their academic careers overseas.

This is not unusual in a part of the world (east from Istanbul) where educational attainment is prized and the title of Dr. elevates one's social standing. It's their last week, in fact they've really already left but at my prompting our sponsor agrees that I should have a discussion with them with the aim of:

- Identifying the networks of people within... who the leavers connected with

- Getting recommendations as to how existing business processes might be enhanced based on experience gained in flagship projects

- Maintaining an ongoing connection with a view to developing an Alumni network of skilled ex ...people

Importance of Set Up

The setup is important. In an environment where conformity and learning by rote the norm everything must be done to make the participants feel at ease and willing to share. Here are six key questions you will need to address:

1. How many in the interview and what are their roles?
2. Where is the interview to be held?
3. Do we record it and get it transcribed. If so how much?
4. How do I catalogue the interview?
5. Where do I store the audio?
6. What will I do with the material?

So the room had to be quiet yet not too formal and the desks set up in a way that encourages conversation not question and answer.

For an interview such as this to really succeed the interviewee needs reflection time. <u>Always send a briefing note</u>, a technique I learned many years ago with Sparknow LLP while conducting an Oral History assignment with Islamic Development Bank.

The purpose of this note is to give an interviewee time to reflect on their career (highs and lows) ahead of their departure, feeling they have said what they want to, been heard and passed on enough that someone following can build on their legacy.

A Few of the Nuggets that Surfaced

In response to the question "what would you tell someone who is taking on the task ...?

- Don't underestimate the challenge of changing mindsets
- Project governance needs to be clear
- Be serious about what is crucial
- Don't just rely on consultants, go find the people who know in our organisation

- Make sure the contract specifically covers who holds the IP rights at the end

- Helping is more important that reporting and always recognise contributions

Each had an anecdote to illustrate it and prompt a meaningful discussion.

A Few Do's and Don'ts

Sudden departures are inevitable in all organizations, those that have processes in place to mitigate such departures will undoubtedly be better off that those who have to react in a hurry. Here's a few do's and don'ts:

- Organizations are usually adept at capturing, don't capture on a just in case basis otherwise you will have created a 'bucket' of information and anecdotes that are never accessed

- Be clear about what it is you are trying to capture and why – it should be the Critical Knowledge that makes the organization work and it would struggle without

- Recognize that when departures do occur you offer the departee an opportunity to leave a legacy and to create an enlarged alumni network.

- Make Knowledge capture and retention part of the way we do things around here, adopting a process that includes learning before, during and after any piece of work and at all stages of the employment cycle

"What's in it for Me": Sharing Client Knowledge across 4 Generations

I'm in Broadgate talking to the Chairman and two Managing Partners of a law firm. There, at the invitation of the Chief Operating Officer, we are discussing inter alia how to deepen relationships so that when the senior relationship manager departs, their knowledge, networks and clients don't depart with them.

'Why Would I Change, There's Nothing in it for Me'

Against a backdrop of increased Mergers & Acquisition activity and potential 'Lift Outs' (hiring of teams from another firm) we talk about why millionaires would share what they know for the benefit of the rest of the firm. I recalled an incident from a previous client, a federation of 13 businesses with very wealthy MD's who had no intention of passing on what they knew about clients or cross selling for the good of the whole firm. This is what one MD said: "I wouldn't let …. anywhere near my client; for a start my business is unique and I don't want them ruining a relationship which has been built up over many years. Ours is a relationship business and I have an assistant who

knows everything about the client and we store all information on the ....
system."

And this from a senior banker: "I have a flat in London and a house in
Umbria. I drive an Aston and the school fees are all paid. Why would I want
to change?"

These are not untypical responses from the upper echelons of
organizations.

Contrast that with a comment from someone I'd describe as *Generation
Rent*, "I have no assets so I go where the excitement is."

How to Cross a Broad Chasm

The proportion of people classed as Generation Rent is predicted to expand
as UK home ownership becomes a distant horizon. This gap isn't going to
close quickly so organizations are relying on squeezed middle management
to be the water carriers between the top and the bottom. For the first time
ever we have 4 generations of workers all working at the same time with
different ways of communicating and working.

In the 'The World Today' Chatham House's bimonthly magazine, there
is a piece on a recent members event during which Kevin Sutcliffe, Head of
News Programming EU, Vice News had this to say:

> There is a notion that television news and documentaries attract an
> older audience. The logic in editorial meetings at Channel 4 News and
> the BBC is that people aged 18-35 aren't interested in the
> world. VICE started to put out documentaries about the coup in Mali
> or the way Egypt and the Arab Spring was unfolding. They were very
> popular. They had engagement times of about 25 minutes and they
> were getting hundreds of thousands of views. So there is great interest
> from that group in the world. The issue was the way it was being
> presented. Most television talks down to people, and that is not
> representative of 16-35 year olds.

In another meeting in The City I was with the KIM Head of a large global
law firm overseeing the process of deepening relationships with clients. He
recognized the need for a meaningful client relationship to be 3 level deep
and the importance of illustrating the differences in the way we all see the
same event or object. His company is getting clients in at 3 levels for show
and tell and share sessions as a way of cementing a relationship and getting
expectations and aspirations out on the table.

Focus on Risk and Assets as a Framework when Thinking about What Critical Knowledge to Keep

What struck a chord during the meetings was the notion of risk – most
organizations understand risk but few set about managing Knowledge in that

context or seeing Knowledge as an asset. While a lot of work has been done on the Risk of Knowledge loss less has been done on the value of Knowledge Assets.

This is how one organization is starting to think about how to contextualize the capture and retention of its Critical Knowledge.

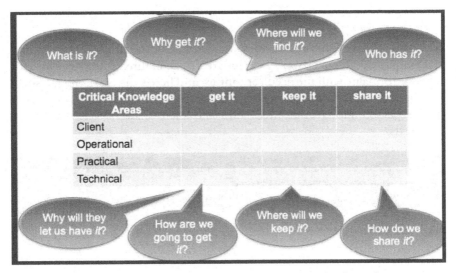

Figure 5-1. Taken from a slide presentation given by the author

This statement (from Harvard Business Review's "Managing your Mission Critical Knowledge" article) sums it up well: "Few companies think explicitly about what knowledge they possess, which parts of it are key to future success, how critical knowledge assets should be managed, and which spheres of knowledge can usefully be combined."

Part 2 - The Tools

A Great Knowledge Capture / Engagement Technique: The Customer Worksheet

My wife Ana recently upgraded her phone as her current contract had expired. Being a born negotiator she always gets a good deal but it's a long process involving a couple of offers from competing suppliers. That brunch on the seafront was mentioned was sufficient for me to tag along. I'm glad I did. Here's why.

We started at EE, Ana's current provider. Friendly and welcoming yes but their approach was "tell me something and I'll fill it onto my system." He was behind a counter and his computer screen was a barrier as was the counter we were sitting at. Ana had to write down what he was saying and ask for a piece of paper to do so. And their offer was appalling.

Next up was phones4u a chain of mobile phone shops. We've been there before and I've always liked their commercial yet subtle sales process which is underpinned by a knowledge capture worksheet (checklist) KM'ers could learn from when they are conducting interviews.

A Checklist that Isn't

It's clever. Every piece of detail the salesman needs to form an opinion about you is there but the overlapping circles are not at all threatening or official. It mixes informality with the need for capture and here's the twist, the salesman can choose which question to pose and when depending on his assessment of the person sitting in front of him and their answers to some of the questions.

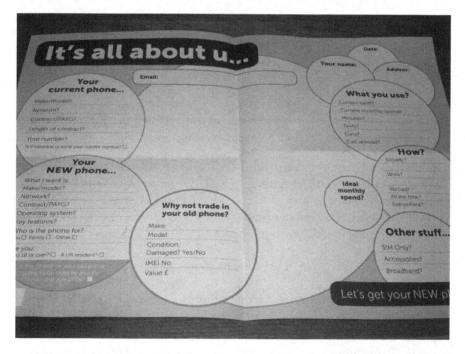

Figure 5-2. Photograph taken by the author with permission of Phones4u

It has 'doodle' space so it feels like a document that is purely for taking notes when actually it is the basis on which their document of record is created.

I asked an experienced salesman who listens – a huge asset, how it differed from their previous checklist. He said and I paraphrase: "The previous form was sequential and official. It pushed you to ask questions in order. This one allows you to move around at a pace that suits the customer and explore areas that they want to discuss."

Why it Works

- Co-created: it feels like a sketch you both create.

- Informal: it encourages you both to scribble – it doesn't feel like it's an official record.

- Personal: It's all about u….is the title and that's how it comes across.

- Structured flexibility: it's an interview spine that in the hands of good interviewers (which is what successful sales people are) provides an insight into a prospective clients' needs against which they can pitch a product.

- Neutral object: we focus on filling in the worksheet not the system – it's a neutral space and so different from the EE approach.

Today reminded me that successfully capturing information and knowledge is very much dependent on the way you go about it. It reinforced the need for good tools and techniques and people well versed in using them and seeing the value in them. phone4u got Ana's business today and they'd get mine next time. As their form says:

"It's all about u…"

The Elephant Fable: A Chinese Reflection on KM, Innovation and Knowledge Capture Techniques

To set the following discussion into context, my name is 'Jonny' Jiang, I am a PhD candidate on service design and service innovation at a design school in London.

I am working part time with Paul at a start-up charity Plan Zheroes to deliver services to make better use of surplus food and help people in food poverty.

Thanks to Paul, I have been given opportunities to learn from his expertise in knowledge management and practice some of his methods to capture knowledge and insights in that charity.

As result, I am able to reflect upon my journey of knowledge management at the charity and my research in service design.

Interestingly, by comparing these two distinctive fields of practices, it gives me some thoughts around the importance of how we can generate new knowledge and insight around innovation.

KM Tools for Learning During and After

Let's talk about some of the knowledge management methods I learnt in this process. Before jumping into these practices, I should tell you I had very little understanding of knowledge management apart from my general reading around business journals.

Paul sat down and demonstrated to me one of the previous knowledge capture sessions he ran with one of the employees at the charity. He explained the rationale of capturing and sharing knowledge among staff through interviews with employees before their leaving and during their life cycle with us.

As I understood, **it is very important to understand each individual's experience and perspectives on his or her journey here and on specific events in particular in order to spot and improve the internal and external operation.**

One of the other rationales I understood very well at the end is Paul's point on the element of constructively **building a better relationship with interviewees even after their leaving to help them reflect upon the personal growth and learning during the period of working inside the organization,** which I realize is very important to each party and helps nurture Alumni Networks.

Later on, I have been given an exercise to listen to Paul's recording on his interview and using his knowledge management toolset (e.g. brief, time map, experience circle, questions) and conclude my findings based on those.

Then a few days after, we sat down again to compare our capture of knowledge based on the same interview and reflected together on some of my questions and learning's. This was an incredibly effective session with Paul because I was able to learn by practice from Paul's expertise to help equip a newbie in knowledge management with knowledge, practical tools and confidence.

I took the lessons and tools from this exercise and conducted an interview with an employee who was about to move to another city and leave the charity. Once the interview was done, I sat down with Paul again to reflect on my interview and report of this knowledge capturing practice.

Most of Paul's methods have been already described and explained very well.

Check out the timeline tool as a way to effectively reflect the knowledge and insights accumulated along the journey. It is a powerful tool because:

- It gives a common language that visually displays our thinking and provokes thoughts around the highlights and lowlights of the journey. In my interview it helped us to reflect on interviewee's expectations at the start of the job, which gives us lots of insights on how we manage the expectation during staff induction.

- Mutually, it also gives an opportunity to help the interviewee consolidate the learning from the job that can be transferred to future careers.

My Elephant and Correlation between Design and Knowledge Management

As Paul invited me to write down my reflections after this exercise, I was fascinated by how similar and powerful the practices around knowledge management and design as a source for organizational innovation can be. As many of us interpret the word 'knowledge' with a connection to 'science' 'scientific' and 'objective', there seems to be a misunderstanding of the value in 'subjectivity' and 'social artefacts'.

As we all come from different experiences in life and become who we are because of those experiences, we all develop very distinctive perspectives on the world based on the things we learnt and have done in the past.

It is like one of the fables I learnt as a child which described four blind people who gave a very different description of the elephant by touching it from their own positions.

Figure 5-3. Made available by S Gross under a creative commons license

Each seems to be fully convinced by their 'objective' interpretation and deny others' views of what the elephant 'truly' is. It is obvious, in the fable, that each of them only 'sees' their part of reality.

In real life, this fable maintains a sense of inspiration too. We all experience a building differently from where we look at it. It can look small from a bird's eye view or intimidating if standing alongside it.

In organizational management nowadays, particularly large organizations, operations can be highly siloed and lack ways of detecting those subtleties in perspectives. It means each department may have their very own budget and competing agenda and develop their very own ways of understanding and doing things under the cover of 'specialization'.

Those silo operations based on 'the only one way' present danger of neglecting the values in perceiving or doing something differently that is at the core of innovation.

As such, knowledge management is becoming increasingly critical to recognize subtlety in each individual's interpretation and map them in order to spot opportunities in the gap of our personal knowledge and experience.

In service design, this idea of interpretation has been very important in user research.

By mapping extensively, designers can understand better the users' perceptions and behaviours and gather deep insights on where the opportunities can be for designing better customer experience and services.

One example of customer journey mapping.

Figure 5-4. Made available by Jenny Cham under a creative commons license.

In Knowledge Management these interpretations can often reveal opportunities and strengths as well as failures and weaknesses.

What Would I Tell Someone about to do the same Knowledge Capture Exercise?

Take the default position of 'he-or-she-knows-much-more-than-me' rather than being judgmental on what you believe as the 'truth' or 'reality'.

As many as we are coming from this global village, there is a great value in the diversity of perspectives and this is where I believe is the infinite source of innovation.

And of course, definitely check out those knowledge management tools on Paul's shelf. They are really effective and surprisingly practical.

In Recognition of my Dad "A Lovely Man": When Knowledge Capture Becomes Personal

John Corney, my Dad, died in August 2015 a month shy of his 87th birthday. Though not unexpected the timing of it was. I was lucky in the sense I got to say goodbye and to reflect while he was still with us on his amazing contribution to and guidance for my own life.

Dad was a 'lovely man' a phrase / tribute we oft heard from those who knew him and a private man. I realized as he neared the end of his life that though we were close there were so many aspects of his background that were opaque to me.

He was of the 'old school' a meticulous senior banker involved in international trade who passionately believed 'my word is my bond' and that debt is a commitment to be honoured. He was not loquacious or a natural storyteller; instead he eschewed the limelight though he was well read, capable of deep insight and eager to debate topics he found stimulating.

For him 'social' was a word associated with a gathering of people not an online activity. Though he recognized the value of the internet, Apps, Smartphones and Tablets were alien concepts to him.

What you might ask has this personal story got to do with business? Here's how:

As Executor of his estate charged with carrying out his wishes I wanted to understand the thinking behind his approach to investment.

I also wanted to understand more about his early life and how he made decisions.

Dad was similar to many senior executives who are often reluctant to acknowledge that their contribution has been significant.

Perhaps subliminally I drew on many of the techniques I encourage others to adopt when trying to capture critical knowledge from people about to retire or relocate:

I used a timeline to look at significant milestones in his life with photos as a prompt:

- We talked about books he had read that had helped shaped his thinking.

- We talked about people he most admired.

- We went through his 'blue book': a transactional history and ledger of all assets.

- We sat and watched something and used that as a neutral space for a conversation.

I spent days ploughing through his archives.

A big regret is that I didn't record any of these discussions but the stories and artefacts remain and I am now their custodian with a duty to pass them onto his great grandchildren so that they too can appreciate John's legacy.

Legacy, What Legacy?

When people leave organizations after a long period legacy is a word often cited as the justification for a knowledge capture interview. What many overlook is the step of thinking up front what is the critical knowledge they are looking to surface during the process.

Often the driver for these initiatives has been a re-organisation, takeover or downsizing; in effect a firefighting exercise.

Setting up a program to consciously capture knowledge is expensive and time consuming: it needs a clear rationale/driver and a set of measurements to track its efficacy and value.

The Power of Postcards

Growing up, one of the chores I associated with holidays was the sending of postcards to family and friends. With no social media or smart phones, we kept in touch via letters and cards. Yet the postcard is still highly effective as it is a tactile, non-technological and versatile object.

Here's a few examples of how I have used it over the past few years:

To Prompt Future Stories

Often at big events (especially the annual corporate '*show and tell*') delegates leave with a list of to do's that few will get done!

At the conclusion of the annual gathering of country heads of a large global charity the delegates were given a postcard with a picture of the venue for next year's event (in this case) Mexico City.

They were asked to write a postcard to themselves saying what they would have done by the time they arrived for next year's gathering.

Here's the instructions we gave them:

> Its 2013 and you are in Mexico at MM13. Imagine you are looking back on a successful year. Write a postcard back to yourself or a friend. Describe a couple of events that took place; things you achieved; things you are proud of.

To Prompt Reflections

As part of an enquiry into the Evolving Role of the Knowledge Manager my colleagues and I at Sparknow wanted to get KIM professionals to chart how their working life has changed over the decade. So we asked people attending the Henley KM Forum to fill in a postcard to themselves to show what's changed. Here's a great response:

> "Hello, we've almost forgotten how to pick up the phone or walk over to speak to people. We spend a lot of time sending "texts" from our phones and reading about our friends' activities from their "electronic" Facebook page. It can be quite lonely at times." Vicki.

To Capture Takeaways from an Event

I was one of the speakers at the inaugural event in Khartoum of the Sudanese Knowledge Society in 2012.

Figure 5-5. Photo taken after Khartoum event and used as a postcard to elicit feedback

The organiser's challenge: how to get people to complete an evaluation without filling in a big form at the event while creating an embryonic community?

The solution: take a group picture and then send it to all the delegates as a virtual (PDF) postcard and ask them to share their takeaways from Khartoum on the reverse.

Here is one of the responses:

> I found strange: being asked to opine on subjects at a moment's notice without any briefing; the sanguine acceptance of 'Africa time'; being called an Australian; and wearing a cap and casual clothes to run a workshop (the closing session).

Part 3 - The Future?

AI Driven Expertise & Profiling: Hype, Hope or Déjà Vu?

May 17 was a busy month. Apart from helping establish then launch a real estate and mortgage business (www.BeesHomes.com) I was in Lisboa for Social Now and London for KM Legal UK.

I attended both in the expectation of learning more about the onrush of Artificial Intelligence and its implications for the Knowledge Management profession.

Specifically, I wanted to see how the encouragingly styled Talent and Knowledge Matching / Profiling systems might tackle the challenges of knowledge loss when people depart, of onboarding when people arrive and identifying / ranking expertise that might otherwise be opaque when pulling together teams.

It's not a new topic: back in the late 90's I was Business & Strategy Advisor to Sopheon PLC when we acquired Organik (a technology for identifying expertise) and built systems for US Insurers looking to establish the best teams for clients based upon expertise. We never cracked it even though we knew what the issues were (usually motivation)!

Armed with a list of 'use cases' I'd worked on with Martin White I set off in search of answers to these questions from both vendors and KM practitioners?

- **Onboarding:** A new employee with many years of highly relevant experience joins the firm. How long will it be before their experience is ranked at the same level as their predecessors?

- **Legal:** Is the profiling process compatible with the provisions of the General Data Protection Regulation? The thoughts of the Information Commissioner on this are worth a look. Profiling & Automated Decision Making

- **Functionality:** Do they offer the ability to present a list of people ranked by expertise?

- **Language:** In multinational companies where it is especially difficult to know all the experts, how does the vendor cope with the fact that documents, meetings and social media traffic will be in local languages?

- **Chinese Walls:** How does the application cope with expertise gained on projects that are secure, a common issue in law, finance and R&D where walls need to be erected to prevent commercial information being divulged

- **Testing:** What User Testing is undertaken with a client before signing a contract to verify that the profiling system works?

Figure 5-6. Photograph of author taken at SocialNow Lisbon interviewing vendors about their expertise systems

So, what did I discover? Thierry de Bailllon in his closing Keynote put it very succinctly but with a caveat: "Embrace or die? 88% of technologies already include AI."

It's not Enterprise Social Networks (ESN)!

This Twitter exchange between Ana Neves and Luis Suarez prompted by a question I posed of the Workplace (Facebook at Work) team following their presentation is revealing:

@ananeves there's been a few questions about expertise location **@SocialNowEvent** 2017 I don't remember that being the case in previous years #**SocialNow**

Luis Suarez @elsua Well, I think people are starting to understand how critical it is to know who is who within the org beyond just content, right? **#socialnow**

@ananeves Replying to **@elsua @SocialNowEvent** totally! It surprises me it took so long. It's amazing the role **#ESN** can have in unveiling that expertise **#SocialNow**

On the surface the case for ESN is compelling. Yet the majority of vendors at SocialNow focus on information exchange and conversation rather than the capturing and cataloguing of it.

One, **@mangoappsinc**, had a neat tool (they won the "coolest app" prize) with the ability to upgrade comments from threaded discussions and posts to create ranked knowledge resources from the mass of information and conversation.

So, ESN can show who has answered what question, conduct searches across conversations and in many cases act as a project management tool, the new Facebook at Work (Workplace) now allows the creation of documents for example.

Provided the application is linked to HR systems it is possible to retrieve profiles and see what expertise an individual might have. As one vendor (**@OrangeTrail** showcasing Facebook at Work)) who uses bots to generate responses put it:

'Questions' is the key to find experts as people don't keep profiles updated.

I concur and they are great facilitation platforms though with advanced features that will suffice for many. Yet I left Lisboa feeling organizations will need to rely on assisted search for some time if they want to take a deep dive into expertise

Should we rely on Emerging Expertise and Profiling Systems?

There are certainly companies who 'get it' but can they do it?

I am indebted here to Martin White who in an excellent report "People and expertise seeking – an overview" summarizes the predicament thus:

> The most important lesson learned is the need for an expertise location strategy that is linked into HR processes, knowledge management, training, job appraisals and social media development. Finding people with expertise is not a 'search problem'. Good search tools can certainly help but without attention being paid to profile quality (even if other types of content are being searched) and a commitment by employees to share their knowledge expertise discovery will not be as successful as anticipated or required.

My takeaways:

- KIM professionals need a clear strategy (working in partnership with other stakeholders such as HR and IT) and be clear on the questions being solved by any system;

- They need to be clear what they are getting, what's missing and how it mitigates the potential for self-reinforcing bias when they enter discussions with vendors around automating expertise seeking and profiling;

- They need to recognize the importance of their role in facilitating the adoption of such systems and accept this is just a part of a portfolio of approaches of identifying, capturing and retaining expertise;

- They need to be clear what critical knowledge actually is in their organisation and who is likely to have it in order to assess the veracity of the results of any pilot;

- It doesn't matter what solution you adopt, if your environment is not conducive to the sharing of expertise and people don't see the value in it then save the money; and

- In any event you cannot capture everything people know; we learn and share through stories (failures rather than successes) and those often remain hidden

ABOUT THE AUTHOR

Paul J. Corney came to knowledge management while working as a Corporate Financier in an Investment Bank in the City of London in the mid-1990s. He is the founder of knowledge et al, a UK-based KM consultancy and former Managing Partner of Sparknow LLP.

He has worked across a variety of sectors in the Americas, Asia, Europe, and the Middle East, helping clients to identify and make use of the knowledge that resides inside their organizations. He recently completed a large project with a major industrial and engineering company, helping them to audit, assess and improve their KM practices, and develop and implement a KM strategy.

Paul is an experienced practitioner, presenter, masterclass leader and lecturer; he chairs international KM conferences, is a visiting lecturer on knowledge and innovation management at the University of Brighton and has published numerous articles one of which was featured in *Making Knowledge Management Work for Your Organization* published by Ark Group in 2012.

His latest book, co-authored with Patricia Eng, is *Navigating the Minefield: A Practical KM Companion* published in May 2017 by the American Society for Quality.

Paul is a member of the British Standards Institute KM Standards committee working on the ISO KM Standard. In 2106 Paul was commissioned by *Business Information Review* to examine the implications of the upcoming standard. Paul found that the adoption of such standards has the potential to become a game changer for KM professionals providing a clear rationale for future KM programmes.

In November 2017 Paul was invited to become a Knowledge & Information Management Ambassador for the Chartered Institute of Library & Information Professionals (CILIP). As a company established by Royal Charter, CILIP is in a unique position to award an independent and unbiased "Chartered Knowledge Manager" accreditation against criteria that should satisfy rigorous examination.

He tweets as @pauljcorney #km4good, blogs at www.knowledgeetal.com and can be contacted at paul.corney@knowledgeetal.com.

CITATIONS & REFERENCES

Generation Rent: Person born in the 1980s who have no hope of getting on the property ladder, a term coined by **The Independent's** Tim Walker.

Henley Forum: Henley Forum for Organizational Learning and Knowledge Strategies located at Henley Business School.

Islamic Development Bank: International Development Institution based in Jeddah owned by many Islamic countries.

KM'ers: Phrase used to denote those who work in the Knowledge & Information profession.

"Managing your Mission Critical Knowledge": **Harvard Business Review** Martin Ihrig & Ian MacMillan January–February 2015 Issue

"People and expertise search – the ultimate challenges in precision and recall?": Martin White **Intranet Focus** Jul 6, 2017

PlanZheroes: UK Charity set up to help make better use of surplus food

SocialNow: annual event organized by Ana Neves of **Knowman** Portugal focusing on the use of Social Enterprise tools.

Sopheon: listed company offering software and services for enterprise innovation management.

Sparknow: UK Management Consultancy that focuses on change.

The World Today: bimonthly magazine published by the **Royal Institute of International Affairs** (Chatham House)

Realize that we as human beings have been put on this earth for only a short time and that we must use this time to gain wisdom, knowledge, respect and the understanding for all human beings since we are all relatives.

~ **Cree Proverb**

COMMUNITIES MANIFESTO

ABOUT THE CHAPTER

Communities are groups of people who, for a specific subject, share a specialty, role, passion, interest, concern, or a set of problems. Community members deepen their understanding of the subject by interacting on an ongoing basis, asking and answering questions, sharing information, reusing good ideas, solving problems for one another, and developing new and better ways of doing things.

People join communities in order to:

1. *Share* new ideas, lessons learned, proven practices, insights, and practical suggestions.
2. *Innovate* through brainstorming, building on each other's ideas, and keeping informed on emerging developments.
3. *Reuse* solutions through asking and answering questions, applying shared insights, and retrieving posted material.
4. *Collaborate* through threaded discussions, conversations, and interactions.
5. *Learn* from other members of the community; from invited guest speakers about successes, failures, case studies, and new trends; and through mentoring.

This chapter defines and describes 10 principles for successful communities. It is based on my experience in creating, leading, and managing communities and communities programs, both inside and outside of organizations.

Acknowledgements

I received very helpful comments and suggestions from Alice MacGillivray, Luis Suarez, Fred Nickols, Bruce Karney, Reed Stuedemann, Lee Romero, and Chris Riemer. I wish to thank them for their guidance.

This chapter is:

Copyright © 2018, Stan Garfield

Please cite as:

Garfield, S. (2018). Communities manifesto. In J. P. Girard & J. L. Girard (Eds.), *Knowledge management matters: Words of wisdom from leading practitioners* (113-127). Macon, GA: Sagology.

6

COMMUNITIES MANIFESTO

BY STAN GARFIELD

10 Principles

1. Communities should be **independent of organization structure**; they are based on what members want to interact on.

2. Communities are different from teams; they are **based on topics, not on assignments.**

3. Communities are not sites, team spaces, blogs or wikis; they are **people who choose to interact.**

4. Community **leadership and membership should be voluntary**; you can suggest that people join, but should not force them to.

5. Communities should **span boundaries**; they should cross functions, organizations, and geographic locations.

6. **Minimize redundancy** in communities; before creating a new one, check if an existing community already addresses the topic.

7. Communities need a **critical mass** of members; take steps to build membership.

8. Communities should start with as **broad a scope as is reasonable**; separate communities can be spun off if warranted.

9. Communities need to be **actively nurtured**; community leaders need to create, build, and sustain communities.

10. Communities can be created, led, and supported using TARGET: **Types, Activities, Requirements, Goals, Expectations, Tools.**

1. Communities should be independent of organization structure. They are based on what members want to interact on.

Some organizations try to align communities to the organization structure. They try to control communities from the top and assign topics, leaders, and membership based on business unit, function, geography, client, market offering, or initiative.

Communities should be based on topics which use easily-recognized terminology, not on organization structure. Communities should be organized around industry-standard, universal topics with which members can identify in their specialties and roles.

Organizations are best served by providing informational sites based on organization structure or internal terminology. These sites are primarily to provide news and content for members of the organization. Communities are best served by providing collaborative capabilities, such as threaded discussion boards and meetings.

2. Communities are different from teams. They are based on topics, not on assignments.

Communities form around people who share a common specialty or interest. Teams share some characteristics, but they are not self-forming. Communities exist to help their members better do their jobs and to deepen their skills and expertise. Teams exist to get work done for the organization. This table compares and contrasts communities and teams.

	Communities	Teams
Purpose	<ul><li>Learning</li><li>Problem-solving</li><li>Innovation</li></ul>	<ul><li>Mission accomplishment</li></ul>
Motivation	<ul><li>Voluntary</li></ul>	<ul><li>Assigned</li></ul>
Duration	<ul><li>Ongoing</li></ul>	<ul><li>Finite</li></ul>
Interaction	<ul><li>Asking and answering questions</li><li>Sharing knowledge</li><li>Reusing good ideas</li><li>Solving problems for one another</li><li>Brainstorming new ideas</li></ul>	<ul><li>Sharing documents and files</li><li>Using a shared calendar</li><li>Attending regular conference calls and meetings</li><li>Maintaining a list of team members</li><li>Editing shared documents</li></ul>
Alignment	<ul><li>Practice</li><li>Interest</li></ul>	<ul><li>Responsibility</li></ul>

Teams include the following types:

1. Work or operating unit
2. Task force
3. Committee
4. Initiative
5. Project

3. Communities are not sites, team spaces, blogs or wikis. They are people who choose to interact.

Community sites are different from team sites, collaborative team spaces, organizational intranet sites, and standalone blogs and wikis. Community sites may use collaboration spaces, blogs, and wikis, but these tools are merely supporting the members, not defining them.

Communities are not the same as social networks, readers of the same blog, or editors of the same wiki page. Such groups of connected people lack some of the fundamental requirements for communities (see section 10).

Communities are made up of people and are supported by processes and technology. You can have a community with no technology at all, but most communities are well-served by using the SCENT tools - Site, Calendar, Events, News, Threads (see section 10).

4. Community leadership and membership should be voluntary. You can suggest that people join, but should not force them to.

Community leaders need to volunteer, not be assigned. Members need to join voluntarily, not be assigned without their permission. People want to exercise their own discretion on which communities to join, whether or not to join, and when to join. They will resent being subscribed by someone else and will resist attempts to make them do something they did not choose to do.

The passion of the leaders and members for the topic of the community is what sustains it. When people are told to lead or join a community and they lack the desire to do so, the community is unlikely to hold events, conduct stimulating discussions, or maintain interest of the members. To entice members to join communities, the leaders should make membership appealing. Create communities for which potential members want to be included in discussions, meetings, and other interactions - make it so they don't want to miss out on what is going on.

Leaders need to meet the SHAPE expectations and members need to perform the SPACE activities (see section 10). Both are more likely to happen if voluntarily agreed to.

5. Communities should span boundaries. They should cross functions, organizations, and geographic locations.

Communities should generally be open to any person aligned with the defined purpose of the community. By transcending organizational structures and boundaries, communities take advantage of diverse experiences, perspectives, and talents.

Those who wish to start a community frequently assert that it is just for one business unit, location, language, or role. For example, a product-focused community that is just for technical people, not sales or marketing people. There may be discussions which are of greater interest to the technical people, but there are also customer problems which the sales people may encounter which may be solved by the technical people. Or there may be technical discussions which can help the marketing people become more knowledgeable.

Another example is a community which is set up in one country and wants to limit membership to that country. This would deny the possibility of people from other countries learning from or contributing to the community. In general, keeping out people who could benefit from membership and offer help to those already in the community hurts both groups.

When I launched the SIKM Leaders Community in 2005, it was intended for KM leaders at consulting and systems integration firms, hence the title of SIKM. It soon became apparent that there was nothing being discussed that could not be of benefit to any KM practitioner, and so the scope was broadened to include anyone who is part of a knowledge management initiative. The benefits of being more inclusive have been many, including a wider range of presenters on the monthly calls, participants in the online discussions, experiences, and perspectives.

6. Minimize redundancy in communities. Before creating a new one, check if an existing community already addresses the topic.

Some people believe that all social media should be offered on a self-serve basis and that anyone should be able to create a new community of practice. Unlike team sites, collaborative team spaces, blogs, wikis, and other social media, the creation of new communities should be reviewed by a coordinating group.

Reviewing requests for new communities has these benefits:

1. Redundant communities can be prevented.
2. A central directory of communities can be maintained, helping potential members find the right ones to join.
3. By keeping the number of communities to a reasonable minimum, a long and confusing list for users to choose from is avoided.

4. Silos which isolate people who could benefit from being connected are avoided.

5. Critical mass is achieved, helping to ensure that each community succeeds and takes advantage of scale (see section 7).

When I took over the HP KM program, there was a very long and bewildering list of communities, most of which were inactive. Potential members could not easily determine which communities were alive and which were dead, and as a result, didn't join any. By deleting the dead ones, creating a streamlined list, and reviewing requests for new ones, the communities program completely turned around and took off.

Most requests for new communities which address a topic already covered by an existing one should be responded to by suggesting that the requester become a co-leader of the existing one. This harnesses the requester's enthusiasm, injects new energy into the existing community, and prevents the fragmentation of members into isolated silos.

7. Communities need a critical mass of members. Take steps to build membership.

A community usually needs at least 100 members, with 200 being a better target. Why should there be at least 100 people? In a typical community, 10% or fewer of the members will tend to post, ask questions, present, etc. If a community has only 10 members, that means that only one person will be doing most of the activity. In a community of 100, you can expect around 10 people to be very active, and that is probably the minimum number for success. As the community grows in size, it becomes more likely that experts belong, that questions will be answered, and that a variety of topics will be discussed.

The greater the number of members in a community, the greater the potential benefit. A community benefits from a broad range of perspectives. If it has only a small number of like-minded members, it is unlikely that innovative ideas, lively debates, and breakthrough thinking will result.

The rule of thumb is that 10% of the members will participate at all, and only 1% will regularly be active in discussions and presentations. In small communities, 1% can be rounded to zero. If only a handful of people speak up, that will not usually sustain momentum.

The larger the membership, the more likely that any question posed to the community will be answered. By including as much of the available expertise as possible in the community, its ability to respond increases accordingly.

Increasing the size of a community yields more potential speakers at community events and conference calls. It results in greater leverage, since for the same effort, more people realize the benefits. And it helps more people to become comfortable in the community model, which can lead them to join other communities, recruit new members, and launch related communities of interest.

8. Communities should start with as broad a scope as is reasonable. Separate communities can be spun off if warranted.

Try to avoid parochialism. Local organizations tend to think of creating local communities and sharing within them, but are reluctant to expand to a global community. Encourage communities to be broader and to include other countries, other parts of the organization, customers, partners, and former employees. This may be hard to sell, even though wider membership will probably make the communities more successful by supplying more answers to questions, additional perspectives, and more varied experience.

Rules of Thumb:

1. Initially, the broadest possible approach to a new community should be supported, and narrowing either by geography or function should be discouraged.
2. Local chapters can be created as subsets of larger communities.
3. Start with the broadest feasible topics, and narrow down as needed.
4. Spin off narrower sub-topics only when a high volume of discussion or communication makes it necessary.
5. Suggest that overlapping communities with similar topics be combined, either directly or with one as a subset of the other.

Challenge those with a niche topic to prove that it warrants its own community:

1. Start as part of a broader community, play an active role in leading discussions and events, and prove a high level of interest.
2. If the volume of activity becomes high, spin off a separate community.
3. If the volume of activity does not become high, remain in the community until it does.

9. Communities need to be actively nurtured. Community leaders need to create, build, and sustain communities.

The first thing to do is to decide what topic you wish to address in a community. Pick a compelling topic that will be of interest to many people in your organization. The potential members must be passionate about the subject for collaboration, and it must be relevant to their work.

You need a committed leader for the community. Volunteer to be the community leader, or identify someone else with the right attributes. The community leader should know the subject, have energy for stimulating collaboration, have sufficient time to devote to leadership, and then regularly spend time meeting the SHAPE goals - Schedule, Host, Answer, Post, Expand (see section 10).

If communities already exist in your organization, then get the answers to these questions:

1. Is your topic already covered as part of another community? If so, offer to help the leader of that community.

2. Is there an existing community that is focused on a related topic? If so, approach its leader about expanding it to include your topic.

3. Is there an old community that is inactive but could be resurrected or migrated to form the new community? If so, ask if you can take over the leadership, or harvest the membership list to start the new one.

Try to take advantage of existing networks:

1. Is there an existing team that could be the core of a new community? For example, is there a team whose mission aligns with the topic for the new community? If so, these can be the initial members.

2. Is there an existing distribution list of people interested in the topic? If so, use that list to invite people to join your community.

3. You can use Social Network Analysis to identify people who are linked but who may not be part of a formal community. Then invite them to join your community.

Once your community is established, publicize its existence to help recruit new members:

1. Write and submit articles to existing newsletters that reach your target audience.

2. Use existing networks to inform possible members about your community.

3. Send a one-time broadcast message to the entire population containing your target audience.

4. Request that links to your community be added on all relevant web sites.

5. Offer an incentive to join, e.g., a member will be chosen at random or the 100th member will receive an iPad or equivalent gift.

Keep the community active:

1. Implement and manage the SCENT tools - Site, Calendar, Events, News, Threads (see section 10).

2. Perform the SHAPE tasks - Schedule, Host, Answer, Post, Expand (see section 10).

3. Regularly suggest to those with questions or interest in your topic that they join the community and use its tools.

Here are some suggestions for helping to develop good community leaders:

1. Suggest to new community leaders that they join a few established communities to observe how they are led and to follow their examples.

2. Lead a community for community leaders and encourage novice community managers to join and participate. Use this community for two main purposes: to share ideas, tips, tricks, and proven practices; and to provide a working example of a community which the members can apply to their communities. Ask the leaders of all communities to take turns presenting on community calls to show how they lead their communities, ask for advice, and share useful insights. Encourage members to post to the community threaded discussion board to ask questions, share knowledge, and practice threaded discussions.

3. Provide recorded training, reading materials, and one-on-one coaching (upon request).

4. Invite speakers from other organizations to tell their stories about communities to your community leaders. Often there is great interest in hearing from fresh, outside voices, so take advantage of this.

5. Have members of the KM Program team or CoP Program team join new communities to observe their activities and discussions. Offer positive reinforcement (i.e., praise) and helpful suggestions (not criticisms) to the leaders.

After a community has been created and developed, it must be nurtured carefully so that it doesn't stagnate or die. Here are some practical tips for how to sustain communities.

Don't let a few members dominate. Encourage lurkers when they surface with an occasional post. Invite a variety of members to speak during calls and meetings. Publicize contributions from all members.

Meet in person, either in a periodic community meeting, or as part of another meeting or training session. Colleagues who see each other regularly are more likely to ask one another for help and to trust one another enough to share documents and other content. Someone who works in the cube next to another person will be likely to visit that colleague to ask for help, to bounce ideas off them, or to ask if they have a document that they can use. They are much less likely to post to a threaded discussion or to contact someone they don't know personally. Face-to-face meetings help overcome this challenge by introducing members to one another.

Aim for a variety of speakers, topics, and activities. In community events, don't always have a presentation. Sometimes schedule a field trip, a discussion, or a social event. Invite outside speakers who hold the attention of the audience. Introduce new topics into threaded discussions. Inject humor and levity to keep things light.

Add an ask the expert process for the community. A specific way to use threaded discussions effectively is to ensure posted questions are answered. This is a service level agreement associated with threaded discussions that guarantees that if you post a question, you will get a response within 48 hours. That response could be the answer to your question (the preferred result), or it could be that the community is working on it and they'll get back to you later with the answer. Or in some cases, it might be that the community doesn't think it can answer that question. But at least you'll get an answer within a specified time and you'll know whether you need to seek a different avenue.

Finally, some communities need to be allowed to die. If a community has failed to build its membership, no longer has active members, no longer has posts to its threaded discussion board, no longer holds events, or no longer has a viable purpose, the right thing to do is to retire it. Move on to another topic of greater relevance and currency which can attract new members who are passionate about it.

10. Communities can be created, led, and supported using TARGET: Types, Activities, Requirements, Goals, Expectations, Tools.

1. *Types* can be used for describing communities, creating a community directory, and helping users readily navigate to the communities which interest them.

2. *Activities* should be used to explain to community members what it means to be a member of a community and how they should participate.

3. *Requirements* should be used to decide if a community should be created and if it is likely to succeed.

4. *Goals* should be set for communities and progress against those goals should be measured and reported.

5. *Expectations* should be set for community leaders to define their role and to ensure that communities are nurtured.

6. *Tools* should support member interaction.

Types can be used for describing communities, creating a community directory, and helping users readily navigate to the communities which interest them. There are five categories which can be used to describe and organize communities: TRAIL - Topic, Role, Audience, Industry, Location

1. Topic (e.g., Enterprise Applications, Cloud Computing)

2. Role (e.g., Project Management, Software Development)

3. Audience (e.g., Recruits, Women)

4. Industry (e.g., Manufacturing, Telecommunications) or Client (e.g., European Union, US Federal Government)

5. Location (e.g., US, UK)

Activities should be used to explain to community members what it means to be a member of a community and how they should participate. There are five ways community members should participate: SPACE - Subscribe, Post, Attend, Contribute, Engage

1. Subscribe: Get email, RSS, or mobile notifications and regularly read a threaded discussion board

2. Post: Start a new thread or reply in a threaded discussion board

3. Attend: Participate in community events

4. Contribute: Submit content to the community newsletter, blog, wiki, or site

5. Engage: Ask a question, make a comment, or give a presentation

Requirements should be used to decide if a community should be created and if it is likely to succeed. There are five elements that communities need: SMILE - Subject, Members, Interaction, Leaders, Enthusiasm

1. Subject: A specialty to learn and/or collaborate about

2. Members: People interested in the subject

3. Interaction: Meetings, calls, and discussions

4. Leaders: People passionate about the subject who are dedicated to creating, building, and sustaining a community

5. Enthusiasm: Motivation to engage and spend time collaborating and/or learning about the subject

Goals should be set for communities and progress against those goals should be measured and reported. Unhealthy communities should either be nurtured back to health or retired. There are five ways to measure the success of a communities program: PATCH - Participation, Anecdotes, Tools, Coverage, Health

1. Participation: % of target population which is a member of at least one community

2. Anecdotes: % of communities displaying the following on their sites:

   a. Testimonials by community members on the value of participation

   b. Stories about the usefulness of the community

   c. Posts thanking other members for their help

3. Tools: % of communities having all five key tools (see below)

4. Coverage: % of desired topics covered by at least one community

5. Health: % of communities meeting these criteria:

a. At least one post to a threaded discussion board per week

b. At least one newsletter or blog post per month

c. At least one conference call, webinar, or face-to-face meeting per quarter

d. At least 100 members

e. At least 10 members participating in each event

Expectations should be set for community leaders to define their role and to ensure that communities are nurtured. There are five tasks for community leaders: SHAPE - Schedule, Host, Answer, Post, Expand

1. Schedule: Line up speakers and set up events

2. Host: Initiate and run conference calls, webinars, and face-to-face meetings

3. Answer: Ensure that questions in the threaded discussion board receive replies, that discussions are relevant, and that behavior is appropriate

4. Post: Share information which is useful to the members by posting to the community site, threaded discussion board, blog, and/or newsletter

5. Expand: Attract new members, content contributions, and threaded discussion board posts

Tools should support member interaction. There are five key tools for communities: SCENT - Site, Calendar, Events, News, Threads

1. Site: home page - for reaching new members and sharing information with current ones

   a. Prominently display most useful content

   b. Update regularly

   c. Make it easy to navigate and visually appealing

   d. Provide obvious links to all important elements

   e. Aggregate multiple sources of relevant information

2. Calendar: of community events - for promoting interaction

   a. Show all scheduled events with details on speakers and topics

   b. Include logistics details such as dial-in numbers

   c. Link to slides and recordings

   d. Include archive of previous events

   e. Schedule recurring events on predictable days and times

3. Events: meetings, conference calls, webinars - for interacting personally
   a. Recurring conference call: 60-90 minutes, held biweekly or monthly
   b. Send out a recurring meeting invitation to lock into members' calendars
   c. Content
      i. Avoid formal organizational announcements and anything else perceived as boring by the members
      ii. Host both internal and external speakers
      iii. Hold a member roundtable and Q&A
      iv. Introduce members to one another to build relationships
      v. Suggest to those who want to present or demo to one member or to a small group that they do so on a call instead
   d. Record the calls and post recordings on the community site and link to in the newsletter or blog
   e. Hold a face-to-face meeting at least once a year
4. News: newsletter or blog - for ongoing communications and publicity
   a. Newsletters should be one page
   b. Leave out boring announcements
   c. Avoid jargon
   d. Link to longer articles
   e. Recognize the members and their contributions
5. Threads: threaded discussion board - for interacting virtually
   a. Post at least once a week to the threaded discussion board
   b. Include a summary of a community event, a useful link, or a thought-provoking topic to stimulate discussion
   c. Look for relevant discussions that are taking place in email exchanges, distribution lists, or outside of the organization
   d. Then redirect those discussions to the threaded discussion board, copy or link to the key points, or summarize the highlights
   e. Regularly suggest to those with questions or interest in the topic that they join the community and post to the threaded discussion board.

ABOUT THE AUTHOR

Stan Garfield is a knowledge management author, speaker, and community leader based in Northville, Michigan. He has worked in the field of knowledge management for over 20 years.

Stan spent 8 years at Deloitte leading communities and enterprise social networking. Prior to that, he spent 25 years at HP, Compaq, and Digital Equipment Corporation. Stan launched Digital's first knowledge management program in 1996, helped develop the corporate KM strategy for Compaq, and led the Worldwide Consulting & Integration Knowledge Management Program for HP. He also worked for PricewaterhouseCoopers, St. Louis University School of Medicine, and Washington University School of Medicine.

Stan holds a BS in Applied Mathematics and Computer Science from Washington University in St. Louis. He leads the SIKM Leaders Community with over 700 members globally, and is invited to present at numerous conferences, including KMWorld. Stan has published over 180 LinkedIn articles on leadership, innovation, knowledge management, communities of practice, enterprise social networks, and social media.

Books:

1. Implementing a Successful KM Program (2007)

2. Successful Knowledge Leadership: Principles and Practice (2013), Chapter 5: The Modern Knowledge Leader: A Results-Oriented Approach

3. Gaining Buy-in for KM (2014), **Chapter 2:** Obtaining support for KM: The ten commitments

4. Measuring the ROI of Knowledge Management (2016), Chapter 7: The case against ROI for knowledge management

5. Proven Practices for Promoting a Knowledge Management Program (2017)

Links:

1. KM Site: http://sites.google.com/site/stangarfield/

2. Posts about Communities: http://bit.ly/2E1GdNu

3. LinkedIn Profile: http://www.linkedin.com/in/stangarfield/

4. Twitter Handle: @stangarfield

Knowledge that is not used is abused.

~ **Cree Proverb**

KNOWLEDGE MANAGEMENT AND BIG DATA

ABOUT THE CHAPTER

The proliferation of data, information and knowledge has created a phenomenon called "Big Data". Knowledge Management when applied to Big Data will enable the type of analysis that will uncover the complete picture of the organization and be a catalyst for driving decisions. The connection between Big Data and Knowledge Management brings together the entirety of your organization's structured and unstructured data sources that are spread across a wide variety of repositories, databases, data warehouses and content sources; in order for your organization to tap into its vast know-how to make better decisions on a multitude of issues and directions on an ongoing basis.

Currently, the ability for an organization to tap into its Big Data sources to gain a competitive edge places a heavy reliance on analytics. Organizations are investigating ways to efficiently and effectively collect and manage the data, information and knowledge they are exposed to various internal and external sources (which are typically networked together). KM will bring opportunities both technical and organizational when working with Big Data. Organizationally KM delivers strategy, governance, process centric approaches and inter-organizational aspects of decision support as well as technical considerations when incorporating new data sources and new frameworks for big data analytics, including knowledge management.

This chapter looks into where Knowledge Management (KM) and Big Data is going within the organization. The advancement of search technologies (which play a key role in delivering knowledge within a knowledge management system) impact our ability to access Big Data and will be examined here. In addition to search several other KM technologies are addressing Big Data. These technologies include solutions that mine unstructured data and manage and use/reuse the knowledge found in Big Data. This chapter will examine knowledge classifications, social network analysis, Big Data sources and information architecture all aimed at providing details on how KM is and will work with Big Data.

This chapter originally appeared in the book *Knowledge Management in Practice* (ISBN: 978-1-4665-6252-3) published by Taylor & Francis Group, LLC

This chapter is:

Please cite as:

Rhem, Anthony J. (2018). Knowledge management and big data. In J. P. Girard & J. L. Girard (Eds.), *Knowledge management matters: Words of wisdom from leading practitioners* (129-150). Macon, GA: Sagology.

7

KNOWLEDGE MANAGEMENT AND BIG DATA

BY ANTHONY J RHEM

A goal of knowledge management is to capture and share knowledge wherever it resides in the organization. Leveraging the corporate collective know-how will improve decision making and innovation where it is needed. The proliferation of data, information and knowledge has created a phenomenon called "Big Data". Knowledge Management when applied to Big Data will enable the type of analysis that will uncover the complete picture of the organization and be a catalyst for driving decisions. In order to leverage an organization's Big Data it must be broken down into smaller more manageable parts. This will facilitate a succinct analysis, which then can be regrouped with other smaller subsets to produce "big picture" results.

Volume, Velocity, and Variety are all aspects that define Big Data.

Volume: The proliferation of all types of data expanding many terabytes of information.

Velocity: The ability to process data quickly.

Variety: Refers to the different types of data (structured and unstructured data such as data in databases, content in Content Management and Knowledge Management systems/repositories, collaborative environments, blogs, wikis, sensor data, audio, video, click streams, log files, etc.).

Variety is the component of Big Data in which KM will play a major role in driving decisions. Enterprises need to be able to combine their analyses to include information from both structured databases and unstructured content.

Data, Information and Knowledge

Since the focus here is about leveraging knowledge management techniques to extract knowledge from Big Data, it is important to understand the difference between data, information and knowledge (see Figure 7-1: Knowledge Management Pyramid). **Data**, I often refer to as being represented by numbers and words representing a discrete set of facts. **Information** is an organized set of data (puts context around data). This can result in an artifact such as a stock report, news article, etc. **Knowledge** on the other hand emerges from the receiver of information applying his/her analysis (aided by their experience and training) to form judgments in order to make decisions. Erickson and Rothberg indicate that information and data only revel their full value when insights are drawn from them (knowledge). Big Data becomes useful when it enhances decision making, which in turn is only enhanced when analytical techniques and an element of human interaction is applied (Erickson and Rothberg, 2014).

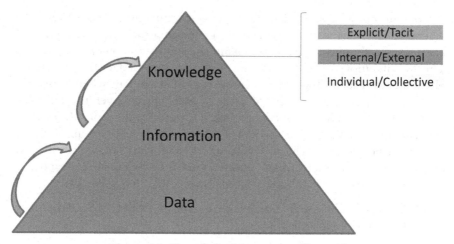

Figure 7-1. Knowledge Management Pyramid

User-generated data

Customers are sharing information about their experience with products and services, what they like and don't like, how it compares to the competition and many other insights that can be used for identifying new sales opportunities, planning campaigns, designing targeted promotions or guiding product and service development. This information is available in social media, blogs, customer reviews or discussions on user forums. Combining all this data contained in call center records and information from other back-office systems can help identify trends, have better predictions and improve the way organizations engage with customers (Andreasen, 2014).

Public data

Public information made available by federal, state and local agencies can be used to support business operations in human resources, compliance, financial planning, etc. Information from courthouse websites and other state portals can be used for background checks and professional license verifications. Other use cases include monitoring compliance regulation requirements, bill and legislation tracking, or in healthcare obtaining data on Medicare laws and which drugs are allowed per state (Andreasen, 2014).

Competitor data

Information about competitors is now widely available by monitoring their websites, online prices, and press releases, events they participate in, open positions or new hires. This data allows better evaluation of the competition, monitor their strategic moves, identify unique market opportunities and take action accordingly. As a retailer for example, correlate this data with order transaction history and inventory levels to design and implement a more dynamic pricing strategy to win over your competition and grow the business (Andreasen, 2014).

Partner data

Across your ecosystem, there are daily interactions with partners, suppliers, vendors and distributors. As part of these interactions organizations exchange data about products, prices, payments, commissions, shipments and other data sets that are critical for business. Beyond the data exchange, intelligence can be gleaned by identifying inefficiencies, delays, gaps and other insights that can help improve and streamline partner interactions (Andreasen, 2014).

To comb through the various sources of user-generated data, public data, competitor data and partner data leveraging KM analytics (data analysis, statistics, and trend analysis) and content synthesis technology (technology that categorizes, analyze, combines, extracts details, and re-assess content aimed at developing new meanings and solutions) will be necessary.

Applying KM to Big Data

The emerging challenge for organizations is to derive meaningful insights from available data and re-apply it intelligently. Knowledge management plays a crucial role in efficiently managing this data and delivering it to the end users to aid in the decision making process. This involves the collection of data from direct and indirect, structured and unstructured sources, analyzing and synthesizing it to derive meaningful information and intelligence. Once this is achieved it must be converted it into a useful knowledge base, storing it and finally delivering it to end users.

Knowledge Management has the ability to integrate and leverage information from multiple perspectives. Big Data is uniquely positioned to take advantage of KM processes and procedures.

These processes and procedures enable KM to provide a rich structure to enable decisions to be made on a multitude and variety of data. In the "KM World March 2012" issue it was pointed out that "organizations do not make decisions just based on one factor, such as revenue, employee salaries or interest rates for commercial loans. The total picture is what should drive decisions". KM enables organizations to take the total picture Big Data provides, and along with leveraging tools that provide processing speed to break up the data into subsets for analysis will empower organizations to make decisions on the vast amount and variety of data and information being provided.

As it pertains to Knowledge Management (KM) and Big Data within organizations, the advancement of search technologies (see Chapter on Big Data is making an impact. In KM World's 100 companies that matter in KM, they point out that Search Technologies' ability to implement, service, and manage Big Data environments is the key reason for their inclusion. The "findability" of information and knowledge within large amounts of unstructured data contribute to the ability to disseminate and reuse the knowledge of the enterprise.

Besides Search Technologies, there are several companies offering KM solutions to address Big Data. Some of these companies include: CACI which offers solutions and services to go from data to decisions, Autonomy (an HP Company) offers KM solutions that mine unstructured data, tag this data and where appropriate make it available to the knowledge base, and IBM who offers a Big Data platform that includes KM to address Big Data's vast amount of unstructured data. As organizations come to know more about Big Data and how to manage and use/reuse the vast amounts of information and knowledge it provides, more software and consulting companies will provide the products and solutions organizations are looking for. Where is Big Data going? A 2013 Gartner Report stated that "Many global organizations have failed to implement a data management strategy but will have to as IT leaders need to support big data volumes, velocity and variety," as well as "decisions from big data projects for decision support, and insights in the context of their role and job function, will expand from 28 per cent of users in 2011 to 50 per cent in 2014."

An emerging opportunity to apply KM to big data will be realized within research institutions (see Chapter 5: The Age of Discovery - KM for Research Institutions). During the innovation activities where product/service development and R&D activities occur; several types of data are generated. Over a period of time this proliferation of data, information and knowledge is created in large volumes, which may be processed and then used/reused within a knowledge repository. This knowledge can be accessed to provide for example; real time intelligence to the research and product development teams, provide knowledge for customer insights as well as competitive intelligence.

Having this access brings about efficiencies in developing new products and services as well as improving existing ones. In order to realize these benefits organizations must start with a well-defined strategy to collect, store, synthesize, and disseminate knowledge in the form of product ideas, customer behavior patterns, Voice of the Customer (VotC), product trends from social networks and listening platforms (among others).

Knowledge, when managed effectively, can help reduce project time, improve product quality, and increase customer satisfaction. In a knowledge-based organization, it plays a crucial role in guiding the organization's actions and establishing a sustainable competitive advantage. The data and information that resides in the systems of the organization, if integrated can create a significant Big Data opportunity that the organization can leverage to create value. This is accomplished through establishing platforms for collaboration between a variety of groups (employees, suppliers, customers and other stakeholders). This collaboration links useful knowledge obtained through Big Data analysis with rules, logic etc. that will help deliver knowledge faster at the right time and in the right content. Leveraging KM with Big Data analysis will also lead to a correct-the-first time decision making, contain cost, and improve performance within and between your collaborative groups.

Social Network Analysis (SNA)

Making sense of large amounts of disorganized information that is spread across the organization has always been the defining challenge of knowledge management. The ability for organizations to capture, analyze and understand information about themselves, their customers and every facet of their business from the various Big Data sources is an ongoing challenge! An important KM tool in aiding organizations to extract knowledge from big data sources is to perform Social Network Analysis (SNA).

Social networks are evolving and growing stronger as forms of organization of human activity. SNA is the mapping and measuring of relationships and flows between people, groups, organizations, computers, URLs, and other connected information/knowledge entities. The nodes in the network are the people and groups while the links show relationships or flows between the nodes. SNA provides both a visual and a mathematical analysis of human relationships. This mapping present nodes of individuals, groups, organizations, and related systems that tie in one or more types of interdependencies: these include shared values, visions, and ideas; social contacts; kinship; conflict; financial exchanges; trade; joint membership in organizations; and group participation in events, among numerous other aspects of human relationships. To understand networks and their participants, we evaluate the location of actors in the network. Measuring the network location is finding the centrality of a node. These measures give us insight into the various roles and groupings in a network. This includes who are the connectors, mavens, leaders, bridges, isolates, as well as where the clusters are and who is in them,

In examining a social network let's look at two (2) nodes that are connected as if they regularly talk to each other, or interact in some way. For example, Tony regularly interacts with Tanya, but not with Sandy. Therefore, Tony and Tanya are connected, but there is no link drawn between Tony and Sandy. This network effectively indicates the distinction between the three most popular individual centrality measures: Degree Centrality, Betweenness Centrality, and Closeness Centrality.

Degree Centrality

Social network researchers measure network activity for a node by using the concept of degrees (the number of direct connections a node has). In the following example, Chris has the most direct connections in the network, making his the most active node in the network. He is a 'connector' or 'hub' in this network. Are more connections better? This is not always true. What really matters is where those connections lead to and how they connect the otherwise unconnected. Here Donald has connections only to others in his immediate cluster -- his clique. He connects only those who are already connected to each other.

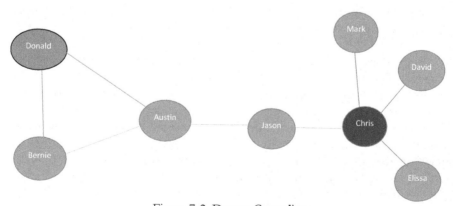

Figure 7-2. Degree Centrality

Betweenness Centrality

While Chris has many direct ties, Jason has few direct connections, yet he has one of the best locations in the network. He is *between* two important constituencies. He plays a 'broker' role in the network. The good news is that he plays a powerful role in the network, the bad news is that he is a single point of failure. Without him, Chris, Elissa, Davis and Mark would be cut off from information and knowledge in Austin's cluster. A node with high betweenness has great influence over what flows and does not flow in the network.

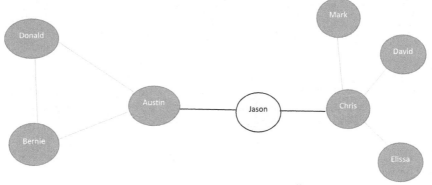

Figure 7-3. Betweenness Centrality

Closeness Centrality

Jason has fewer connections than Chris, yet the pattern of his direct and indirect ties allows him to access all the nodes in the network more quickly than anyone else. He has the shortest paths to all others, and closer to everyone else. He is in an excellent position to monitor the information flow in the network and therefore has the best visibility into what is happening in the network.

Let's take a look at other social network measures that contribute to gaining knowledge from the relationships in your networks. These include: Network Centralization, Network Reach, Network Integration, Boundary Spanners, and Peripheral Players.

Network Centralization

Individual network centralities provide insight into the individual's location in the network. The relationship between the centralities of all nodes can reveal much about the overall network structure.

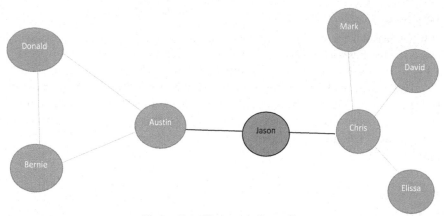

Figure 7-4. Closeness Centrality

A very centralized network is dominated by one or a few very central nodes. If these nodes are removed or damaged, the network quickly fragments into unconnected sub-networks. A highly central node can become a single point of failure. A network centralized around a well-connected hub can fail abruptly if that hub is disabled or removed. Hubs are nodes with high degree and betweeness centrality.

A less centralized network has no single points of failure. It is resilient in the face of many random failures -- many nodes or links can fail while allowing the remaining nodes to still reach each other over other network paths. Networks of low centralization seldom fail.

Network Reach

Not all network paths are created equal. In many instances, the shorter paths in the network are more important (see Figure 7-4. Closeness Centrality). It is also of note that networks have horizons over which we cannot see, nor influence. In these cases the key paths in the network are 1 and 2 steps and on occasions, three steps to all connections (direct and indirect). Therefore, it is important to know: who is in your network neighborhood, who you are aware of, and who can you reach (network reach).

Network Integration

Network metrics are often measured using shortest paths. This measurement makes the (often incorrect) assumption that all information and/or influence flows along the network's shortest paths only. However, networks operate via direct and indirect, shortest and near-shortest paths.

Boundary Spanners

Nodes that connect their group to others usually end up with high network metrics. Boundary spanners such as Austin and Jason are more central in the overall network than their immediate neighbors whose connections are only local, within their immediate cluster. A boundary spanner occurs via your bridging connections to other clusters or via your concurrent membership in overlapping groups. Boundary spanners are well-positioned to be innovators, since they have access to ideas and information flowing in other clusters. They are in a position to combine different ideas and knowledge, found in various places, into new products and services.

Peripheral Players

Most people would view the nodes on the periphery of a network as not being very important. In fact, nodes such as Mark and David receive very low centrality scores for this network. Since individuals' networks overlap, peripheral nodes are connected to networks that are not currently mapped. Mark and David may be contractors or vendors that have their own network outside of the company, making them very important resources for fresh information not available inside the company.

SNA Graph/Knowledge Map

The SNA Graph presents similar information as a Knowledge Map. A SNA Graph is a tool used in Social Network Analysis to represent information about patterns of ties among social actors; while a Knowledge Map is a graphical representation of people in an organization or within a network indicating their expertise and understanding who are the key knowledge holders indicating what knowledge is essential or at risk to be lost if someone is removed from the network/organization.

Social scientists use graphs as a tool for describing and analyzing patterns of social relations. In lieu of taking a deep dive into the specific terminology, presented here will represent some important ideas about social structure in a simpler more consumable manner. Once the basics have been mastered a deeper dive may be in order.

Graph theory provides a set of abstract concepts and methods for the analysis of graphs. This provides a visualization of social (as well as other) networks. As with knowledge maps, SNA Graphs centers on relations between individuals, groups and institutions. In studying a network in this manner we are examining individuals as embedded in a network of relations rather than from an individual basis. Due to the widespread availability of data it is from this basis that SNA can be applied to a range of problems, including analyzing big data.

Social Media Networks

With the popularity of social media many more people and groups are interacting. Through these interactions a proliferation of knowledge is created and shared. Social networks such as LinkedIn, Twitter and Facebook facilitate a key component of knowledge management and that is knowledge sharing. Through these networks a multitude of data can be analyzed that can lead to enhanced decision making in many areas such as product marketing, identifying key thought leaders and decision makers.

Social network analysis is based on an assumption of the importance of relationships among interacting units. The social network perspective encompasses theories, models, and applications that are expressed in terms of relational concepts or processes. Along with growing interest and increased use of network analysis has come a consensus about the central principles underlying the network perspective. In addition to the use of relational concepts, we note the following as being important:

- Actors and their actions are viewed as interdependent rather than independent, autonomous units

- Relational ties (linkages) between actors are channels for transfer or "flow" of resources (either material or nonmaterial)

- Network models focusing on individuals view the network structural environment as providing opportunities for or constraints on individual action

- Network models conceptualize structure (social, economic, political, and so forth) as lasting patterns of relations among actors

The unit of analysis in network analysis is not the individual, but an entity consisting of a collection of individuals and the linkages among them. Network methods focus on dyads (two actors and their ties), triads (three actors and their ties), or larger systems (subgroups of individuals, or entire networks, which social media networks provide.

Big Data Sources & Knowledge Management

The use of Big Data and its analysis is very closely driven by the available technologies in the organization, and the tight integration between hardware and software and other data generation mechanisms. A Big Data strategy requires the ability to sense, acquire, transmit, process, store and analyze the data to generate knowledge that can be stored in a repository for later use.

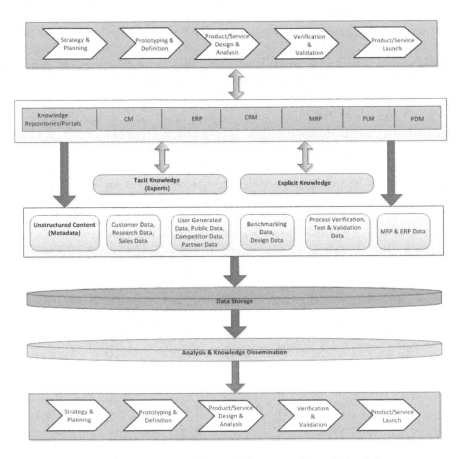

Figure 7-5. Enterprise View of Big Data Sources & Knowledge Management
(based on Rajpathak & Narsingpurkar)

In analyzing Big Data and understanding where knowledge management can play a role starts with analyzing the data, information and knowledge within enterprise-wide systems. These systems include but are not limited to Knowledge Repositories/Portals, Content Management (CM), Enterprise Resource Planning (ERP), Customer Relationship Management (CRM), Material Requirements Planning (MRP), Product Lifecycle Management (PLM) and Product Data Management (PDM) systems (see Figure 7-5. Enterprise View of Big Data Sources & Knowledge Management).

The knowledge that can be gained from these systems include tacit (by identifying the key knowledge holders of the content, which in this reference includes information and knowledge) and explicit (through accessing the various types of Market, Technology, Procedural, Customer and Competitor knowledge that is captured and unstructured (see Table 7-1. Mapping Knowledge Areas to Big Data Elements). Information and data are exchanged on a continuous basis with these systems as the product and services are being realized. The unconventional, unstructured information comes from several sources like simulation, sensors, blogs, employee experience, wikis, customer experience, etc., and it should be harnessed.

Knowledge Classifications

Knowledge, in particular organizational knowledge typically exists in large volumes dispersed across the enterprise. This lends itself to the fact that organizations need to find a way to discover, classify, capture, disseminate and reuse this knowledge. Once the knowledge sources are discovered, an essential element to leverage KM in big data is to classify that knowledge.

According to Yuan, Yoon, and Helendar, knowledge areas are classified into four types, collectively referred to as M-H-T-P: Market knowledge, Human (tacit) knowledge, Technology knowledge, and Procedural (explicit) knowledge. Based on these four knowledge areas, Table 7-1. Mapping Knowledge Areas to Big Data Elements depicts the mapping of knowledge areas with elements of Big Data (Yuan, Yoon, and Helendar, 2006).

Knowledge Type	Volume	Velocity	Variety	Value
Market Knowledge	• Customer Data • Competitor Data • User Generated Data • Public Data • Competitor Data • Partner Data	• Direct Interactions • Social Media • Surveys	• Market Analysis • Demographic Data • Benchmarking Data • Trends	• High Value • Customer Data • User Generated Data • Competitor Data • Partner Data
Human (Tacit) Knowledge	• Experience Based • Collaborative	• Real-time Decision Making	• Skill Based • Experience Based • Tacit Knowledge	• Heuristics
Technology Knowledge	• Standards • Usage • Materials • Field Data	• Real-Time Data Acquisition	• Cost • Reliability • Packaging • Ergonomics	• Patents
Procedural Knowledge	• Design Knowledge • Analysis • Verification, Testing and Validation Knowledge	• Design Knowledge • Knowledge Repository/Knowledge Base	• Procedures • Job-Aids • Workflows	• Best Practices • Process Data • Validation Data

Table 7-1. Mapping Knowledge Areas to Big Data Elements (derived from Yuan, Yoon and Helendar, 2006)

While a small part of this information flows back into the enterprise systems, attempts should be made to capture this in a central repository, typically a single data warehouse. A deliberate attempt must be made to keep the data together so that the data can be combined to create information, which can be analyzed to generate knowledge that loops back to the knowledge repository and into the organization.

Information Architecture and Big Data

As detailed in chapter 4 of *Knowledge Management in Practice*, Information Architecture is the art and science of labeling and organizing information, so that it is findable, manageable and useful (Downey and Banerjee, 2010). Information Architecture also plays a significant role when applying KM to Big Data.

Big Data leverages techniques and technologies that enable enterprise to effectively and economically analyze all of its data. We need to remember that Big Data includes all data (i.e., Unstructured, Semi-structured, and Structured). The characteristics of Big Data (Volume, Velocity, and Variety) are a challenge to your existing architecture and how you will effectively, efficiently and economically process data to achieve operational efficiencies.

In order to derive the maximum benefit from Big Data, organizations must modify their IT infrastructure to handle the rapid rate of delivery and extraction of huge volumes of data, with varying data types. These can then be integrated with the organization's enterprise data and analyzed. Organizations, with legacy systems, must have a clear understanding of their historical data and how that data can be managed as a part of their overall Big Data picture.

Information Architecture provides the methods and tools for organizing, labeling, building relationships (through associations), and describing (through metadata) your unstructured content adding this source to your overall analysis. In addition information architecture enables Big Data to rapidly explore and analyze any combination of structured and unstructured sources. Big Data requires information architecture to exploit relationships and synergies between information, aligning unstructured and structured data. This infrastructure enables organizations to make decisions utilizing the full spectrum of your big data sources.

To facilitate the inclusion of unstructured data (content) the metadata schema must be utilized (it is developed as a part of the information architecture). Having a sound Information Architecture will enable a consistent structure to big data in order for this data to provide value to the organization. The Enterprise Information Architecture Checklist will assist in enabling a consistent structure.

BIG Data Components

Information Architecture Elements	Volume	Velocity	Variety
Content Consumption	Provides an understanding of the universe of relevant content through performing a content audit. This contributes directly to volume of available content.	This directly contributes to the speed at which content is accessed by providing initial volume of the available content.	Identifies the initial variety of content that will be a part of the organization's Big Data resources.
Content Generation	Fill gaps identified in the content audit by Gather the requirements for content creation/ generation, which contributes to directly to increasing the amount of content that is available in the organization's Big Data resources.	This directly contributes to the speed at which content is accessed due to the fact that volumes are increasing.	Contributes to the creation of a variety of content (documents, spreadsheets, images, video, voice) to fill identified gaps.
Content Organization	Content Organization will provide business rules to identify relationships between content, create metadata schema to assign content characteristic to all content. This contributes to increasing the volume of data available and in some ways leveraging existing data to assign metadata values.	This directly contributes to improving the speed at which content is accessed by applying metadata, which in turn will give context to the content.	The Variety of Big Data will often times drive the relationships and organization between the various types of content.
Content Access	Content Access is about search and establishing the standard types of search (i.e., keyword, guided, and faceted). This will contribute to the volume of data, through establishing the parameters often times additional metadata fields and values to enhance search.	Contributes to the ability to access content and the speed and efficiency in which content is accessed.	Contributes to how the variety of content is access. The Variety of Big Data will often times drive the search parameters used to access the various type of content.
Content Governance	The focus here is on establishing accountability for the accuracy, consistency and timeliness of content, content relationships, metadata and taxonomy within areas of the enterprise and the applications that are being used. Content Governance will often "prune" the volume of content available in the organization's Big Data resources by only allowing access to pertinent/relevant content, while either deleting or archiving other content.	When the volume of content available in the organization's Big Data resources is trimmed through Content Governance it will improve velocity by making available a smaller more pertinent universe of content.	When the volume of content available in the organization's Big Data resources is trimmed through Content Governance the variety of content available may be affected as well.

BIG Data Components

Information Architecture Elements	Volume	Velocity	Variety
Content Quality of Service	Content Quality of Service focuses on security, availability, scalability, usefulness of the content and improves the overall quality of the volume of content in the organization's Big Data resources by: - defending content from unauthorized access, use, disclosure, disruption, modification, perusal, inspection, recording or destruction - eliminating or minimizing disruptions from planned system downtime making sure that the content that is accessed is from and/or based on the authoritative or trusted source, reviewed on a regular basis (based on the specific governance policies), modified when needed and archived when it becomes obsolete - enabling the content to behave the same no matter what application/tool implements it and flexible enough to be used from an enterprise level as well as a local level without changing its meaning, intent of use and/or function - by tailoring the content to the specific audience and to ensure that the content serves a distinct purpose, helpful to its audience and is practical.	Content Quality of Service will eliminate or minimize delays and latency from your content and business processes by speeding to analyze and make decisions directing effecting the content's velocity.	Content Quality of Service will improve the overall quality of the variety of content in the organization's Big Data resources through aspects of security, availability, scalability, and usefulness of content.

Table 7-2. Information Architecture Elements Align to Big Data

Elements of the Enterprise Information Architecture Checklist include; Content Consumption, Content Generation, Content Organization, Content Access, Content Governance and Content Quality of Service. It is this framework (see Table 7-2. Information Architecture Elements Aligned to Big Data Components) that will align your information architecture to big data which will provide business value to be gained from all of your Big Data resources.

Some of the essential elements of the information architecture as it pertains to Big Data include:

1. Content Consumption, which provides an understanding of the universe of relevant content through performing a content audit. This contributes directly to volume of available content.

2. Content Generation, which fills gaps identified in the content audit by gathering the requirements for content creation/generation. This in turn will contribute directly to increasing the amount of content that is available in the organization's Big Data resources.

3. Content Organization will provide business rules to identify relationships between content, create metadata schema to assign content characteristic to all content. This contributes to increasing the volume of data available and in some ways leveraging existing data to assign metadata values.

4. Content Access is all about search and establishing the standard types of search (i.e., keyword, guided, and faceted) that will be needed. This will contribute to the volume of data, through establishing the parameters and often times additional metadata fields and values to enhance search.

5. Content Governance focuses on establishing accountability for the accuracy, consistency and timeliness of content, content relationships, metadata and taxonomy within areas of the enterprise and the applications that are being used. Content Governance will often "prune" the volume of content available in the organization's Big Data resources by only allowing access to pertinent/relevant content, while either deleting or archiving other content.

6. Content Quality of Service, which focuses on security, availability, scalability, usefulness of the content and improves the overall quality of the volume of content in the organization's Big Data resources by:

   a. defending content from unauthorized access, use, disclosure, disruption, modification, perusal, inspection, recording or destruction

   b. eliminating or minimizing disruptions from planned system downtime making sure that the content that is accessed is from and/or based on the authoritative or trusted source, reviewed on a regular basis (based on the specific governance policies), modified when needed and archived when it becomes obsolete

   c. enabling the content to behave the same no matter what application/tool implements it and flexible enough to be used from an enterprise level as well as a local level without changing its meaning, intent of use and/or function

   d. by tailoring the content to the specific audience and to ensure that the content serves a distinct purpose, helpful to its audience and is practical.

Inclusion of additional types of data into the information architecture is needed. This includes semi-structured data (i.e., data coming from sensors such as RFID, location information coming from the mobile devices, information from web logs. documents and emails). These new data elements are often produced at much higher rates than the classical transactional data. There is a lot more data coming in at much higher rates, and enterprises need to be able to manage these new types of data and incorporate them into their overall information architecture framework. These new types of data are one of the new characteristics of big data.

Key Learning's:

The following represents key learnings from KM and Big Data:

1. Don't repeat solving the same problem. Perform root-cause analysis and focus your analytics to solve the "right problem"!

2. The same principle that knowledge still exists within an organization's data still holds, however the challenge is to manage the knowledge found by breaking it down into smaller consumable "chunks" and then bring them together to form a complete picture.

3. There must be a culture change which will enable the belief that all of the individuals in an organization are owners of both their own and the company's knowledge.

4. Workers today must be coached to manage, organize and take responsibility (or held accountable) for their content (information and knowledge) that they create at every step of their work process.

5. Principles of knowledge management are scalable as data grows.

6. The security, availability, scalability, usefulness of the content can only be achieved by executing a comprehensive Content and Data Governance Strategy.

Tips & Techniques:

The following represents tips & techniques from KM and Big Data:

1. Leverage Big Data tools such as Apache's Hive, Mahout and Hadoop to bring significant value to your Big Data analytics, which include but are not limited to:

   a. Detecting abnormal behavior patterns

   b. Detecting trends through social media activities

   c. Detecting suspicious activities

   d. Identifying discrepancies in records across systems

2. Aligning your organizations tacit knowledge (experts) to content (information and knowledge) through expertise locators, assignment of authoritative voice as a metadata field/value is an essential part of extracting knowledge from your Big Data sources.

3. Include in your Big Data knowledge extraction efforts the understanding of the data, information and knowledge within your enterprise-wide systems and the specific knowledge types that are important to your organization to capture.

4. Create a comprehensive information architecture structure in order to enable unstructured data to be included into the mix of Big Data sources.

5. Alignment of information architecture elements with big data components will enable consistencies when including unstructured data to the organizations big data environment.

ABOUT THE AUTHOR

Dr. Anthony J Rhem, PhD., is an Information Systems professional with over thirty (30) years of experience. Since 1990 Dr. Rhem has served as President/Principal Consultant of A.J. Rhem & Associates, a privately held knowledge management and system integration consulting, training & research firm located in Chicago, Illinois. As a consultant, strategist and advisor Dr. Rhem has worked with United States fortune 500 corporations in retail, communications, financial, insurance, legal, and healthcare; as well as educational institutions and the military (US Army and US Air Force) in implementing strategies, policies and solutions centered on information technology and Knowledge Management (KM).

Dr. Rhem consults with venture capitalist and investment firms specifically as it pertains to technology innovations, best practices and trends. As an advisor Dr Rhem's work includes participating on the Corporate Advisory Board for the ASCII Group, Chairman - Board of Trustees Knowledge Systems Institute, Industry Advisory Board – International Conference on Software Engineering and Knowledge Engineering (SEKE), Technology Council of Advisors Gerson Lehrman Group (GLG), Chair of the International Bar Association (IBA) Law Firm Management Working Group on Knowledge Management and IT, and Member of the National Science Foundation SBIR (Small Business Innovative Research) Review Panel in the areas of AI, KM, Big Data and Education.

As a professor and corporate Instructor, Dr Rhem has had the pleasure of training hundreds of personnel across many organizations in the principles, practice and application of strategic management, software engineering, knowledge management and information architecture. Considered a thought leader in KM, Dr. Rhem is an active presenter at KM conferences both domestic and international, and continues to write articles and books in KM. His blog The Knowledge Management Depot was recognized as a must read by EditorEye for CIO's in 2015.

Dr. Rhem's educational background includes: Walden University, Ph.D. Knowledge Management; Dartmouth University Tuck School of Business, Advance Executive Management Training; Clark Atlanta University, Executive Management Training; DePaul University, M.S. Information Systems/AI; Purdue University, B.S. Marketing/Computer Science; Certified Knowledge Manager (CKM), Knowledge Management Institute; Certified SCRUM Master, Agile University and Certified ITIL Foundations, EXIN. His books include: Globe Law and Business "Knowledge Management in Law Firms", December 2016; CRC Press (Taylor and Francis) "Knowledge Management in Practice" July, 2016; and CRC Press (Taylor and Francis) "UML for Developing Knowledge Management Systems" Nov 2005..

BIBLIOGRAPHY

Andreasen, S. (2014). Big data delivering big knowledge. *KM World.* http://www.kmworld.com/Articles/Editorial/Viewpoints/Big-Data-Delivering-Big-Knowledge-95057.aspx . Accessed April 18, 2015.

Downey, L., & Banerjee, S. (2011). Building an Information Architecture Checklist. Journal of Information Architecture. Vol. 2, No. 2. [Available at http://journalofia.org/volume2/issue2/03-downey/].

Erickson, S. and Rothberg, H. Big Data and knowledge management: Establishing a conceptual foundation. *The Electronic Journal of Knowledge Management*, Volume 12, Issue 2, pp. 108–116. Available at www.ejkm.com.

Gartner Press Release (Sept 17, 2014). Gartner Survey Reveals That 73 Percent of Organizations Have Invested or Plan to Invest in Big Data in the Next Two Years. http://www.gartner.com/newsroom/id/2848718.

LoPresti, M. (2014). The long tail of knowledge: Big data's impact on knowledge management. http://www.econtentmag.com/Articles/News/News-feature/The-long-tail-of-knowledgebig-datas-impact-on-knowledge-management-96285.htm . Accessed February 4, 2015.

Rajpathak, T. and Narsingpurkar, A. Manufacturing Innovation and Transformation Group (ITG), TCS. Managing Knowledge from Big Data Analytics in Product Development. http://www.tcs.com/resources/white_papers/Pages/Knowledge-big -data-analyticsproduct-development.aspx . Accessed March 2015.

Yuan, Q.F., Yoon, P.C., and Helander, M. G. (2006). Knowledge identification and management in product design. *Journal of Knowledge Management*, Volume 10, Issue 6, pp. 50–63.

TOWARDS KNOWLEDGE ASSET MANAGEMENT

ABOUT THE CHAPTER

I first published an article and an implementation framework entitled ' The Four Dimensions of Knowledge and Innovation' in 2007. This framework is a fundamental part of our Strategic Knowledge Asset Management Methodology (KAM) that we, as Knowledge Associates, teach to KM Practitioners and Consultants around the world. Since then, I have seen such rapid globalization and radically new thinking, knowledge methods, platforms, tools and technologies emerge, to enable far more productive and effective global knowledge working for individuals, teams and entire organizations.

We are now in the era of the empowered 'global individual'. We are now in the era of both human and machine intelligence, and better ways to manage your knowledge assets using blockchain technologies. You might say that today is the 'warm up act' for even faster, more ruthless, knowledge creation and innovation. So, following another 10 years of research and development, workshops, and client implementation experiences across the world, I have now reviewed and updated our implementation framework, which is now entitled 'The Five Dimensions of Knowledge and Innovation – personal, team, organization, inter-organization and global'.

Therefore, the purpose of this chapter is to share further insights and experiences and, most importantly, a better understanding of the inter-relationships between these five critical dimensions leading to successful collaboration, co-creation, learning, knowledge management, strategic knowledge asset management, and innovation.

This chapter is:

Copyright © 2018, Ron Young

Please cite as:

Young, R. (2018). Towards knowledge asset management. In J. P. Girard &
J. L. Girard (Eds.), *Knowledge management matters: Words of wisdom from leading
practitioners* (151-164). Macon, GA: Sagology.

8

TOWARDS KNOWLEDGE ASSET MANAGEMENT

BY RON YOUNG

Over 20 years ago, I was a co-author of a book called 'Upside Down Management – revolutionizing management and development to maximize business success', McGraw-Hill Europe, 1995. At that time, I was concerned that our organizations were too rigid, structured, linear, and too information based, and what we needed to better understand was the need, in a growing highly inter-connected global knowledge society, for our organizations to become more like biological organisms. Organisms are flexible, holistic, fluid, dynamic, and human organisms are adaptive, knowledge driven and knowledge based.

I said in the book, at the time, "People are organisms! People are very complex organisms." Therefore, it has always been obvious to me that limited and structured hierarchical 'organizations' that have been designed to work for a predominantly industrial economy, have never been able, nor never will be able, to develop intelligent organisms, nor enable them to flourish, naturally, to their full potential, to take full advantage of the knowledge economy and the need for effective knowledge asset management, knowledge productivity and innovation. We need new global knowledge driven structures.

Actually, a dictionary definition is that information based organizations are "organized bodies which give orderly structure to components", whereas knowledge driven organisms are entities which take the organized body further by "connecting the parts that are interdependent and share a common life!" I started to look for better ways to develop and apply effective knowledge working competencies within and between people, as more knowledge driven organisms, to help better achieve, or even exceed, the organization's objectives.

My company, Knowledge Associates International, was part of a 2 million euro European Commission funded project and European collaborative research and development consortium, called *Know-net* in the period to 2003, to develop a holistic framework, methods and tools around the concept of Knowledge Asset Management. The detailed research proceedings are published in the book I co-authored entitled *Knowledge Asset Management –* beyond process centred and product centred approaches', Springer 2003.

At that time, we recognized the need to consider strategic and operational knowledge assets as both knowledge flows between people and codified knowledge objects. Current thinking then was that knowledge assets were just codified, and took no proper recognition of the most valuable and powerful knowledge assets of all, the key human knowledge assets such as experts, highly collaborative and co-creative teams, knowledge networks and communities and, the deep inter-relationships between all types of knowledge assets.

Knowledge assets can be human, and they can be codified and embedded in the organizational structures and routines. Also, at that time, there were no effective measurements for strategic and operational knowledge assets. But nonetheless, we had developed and implemented far more effective knowledge working competencies frameworks, systems and tools in organizations around the world. And I was happier with frameworks that were more holistic and far more knowledge asset centric.

But I was still most concerned with the different levels of effective knowledge work within and between knowledge driven and knowledge based organizations. In most organizations, I saw 'organizational' knowledge management initiatives. In many organizations, I saw 'team' knowledge management initiatives. In some organizations, I saw 'personal' knowledge management initiatives and, in some organizations, I saw 'inter-organizational' knowledge management initiatives. All of the above initiatives were very well intentioned, and without doubt, gave some benefit to the organization. But, in all the initiatives I researched, they didn't seem to go any further than one or two dimensions.

What seemed to happen is that a KM strategy was developed along one of these dimensions, as the focus, as the strategic imperative, but there it seemed to end. Then, either the initial KM champion left the organization, or the results from the initiative were found to be mediocre at best, and even failure at worst. I felt that this was very sad indeed. In many instances, I could see that many organizations were clearly 'throwing the baby out with the bathwater'. From the European Commission project Know-Net in 2003, we developed the following holistic, and knowledge asset centric framework that identified, at the time, the four dimensions of knowledge management, as follows:

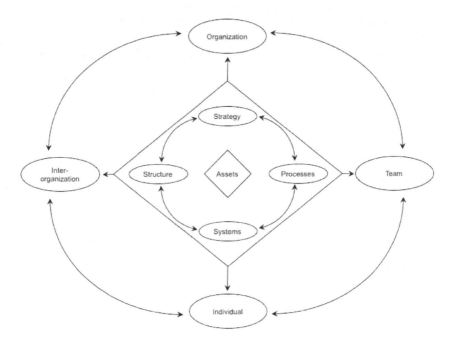

Figure 8-1. Holistic Knowledge Asset Framework
(Adapted from Mentzas et al, 2003, p.25)

The outer ring of the framework is referred to as the 'knowledge networking levels', the interdependencies which facilitate the natural emergence, leveraging, and flow of knowledge and knowledge assets. We recognised at the time, four levels of knowledge networking: individual level, team level, organizational level, and inter-organizational level.

These knowledge networking levels surround the four inner 'KM Infrastructure' components: strategy, structure, processes and systems, which, in turn, surround the organizations key knowledge assets, primarily strategic, but also operational, as the primary focus. It was our strong view that any organization that considered knowledge to be a key asset, or even 'the key asset', needed a compelling and holistic organizational knowledge asset centric framework and strategy to successfully implement the principles, processes, methods, tools and techniques in all of these four knowledge networking levels and dimensions of effective knowledge work. Many organizations have only partially focused on this critical issue to date.

Furthermore, the strategies, processes, methods and tools are situational, that is to say, dependent on their unique objectives, properties, culture, people and technologies, and will, therefore, vary according to each organization, and to each of the four dimensions. There is no magic pill or quick fix, for such a powerful and transformational organizational renewal, and the role of the consultant or practitioner must be to help the organization with its own adaption and implementation of the key principles of knowledge asset management.

In 2010, we further developed these four critical dimensions into five, as below:

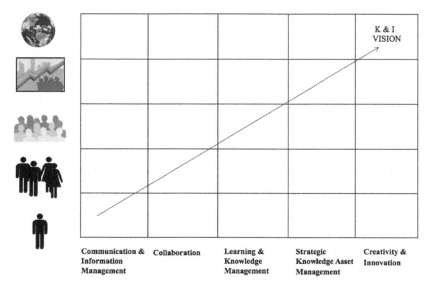

Figure 8-2. The 5 Dimensions of Knowledge & Innovation

Personal Knowledge Management and Innovation

The lower vertical level of the framework represents the personal dimension. A number of organizations have implemented a strategy for personal knowledge management and innovation. This is a 'bottom up' approach and comes from the belief that by improving the personal ability of employees to better identify, capture, store, share and apply their personal knowledge and creativity, this will inevitably result, as an automatic outcome, in better knowledge management and innovation at the higher levels of team, organizational, inter-organizational and global levels.

The other driver for personal knowledge management and innovation is the growing need, for many individuals and organizations, to better tackle 'information overload' and make more sense of our world of increasing complexity, to develop more focus, to become more proactive in task prioritization and decision making, and to better manage time and projects. This also comes from the realization that this will reduce stress, increase personal creativity and productivity, and lead to greatly improved work-life balance.

The personal, or individual level refers to the personal knowledge, capabilities, experiences, competencies, ideas and personal development issues for each individual knowledge worker. Therefore, the strategies, methods and tools used for this dimension are at the personal level, to personally capture, learn, interpret, envision, analyse, synthesize, communicate, create, share and apply knowledge. Personal productivity, knowledge management and innovation, has been greatly accelerated by mobile, wireless and web-based tools such as smart phones, tablets, cameras and camcorders, global positioning tools, personal computers, search engines, tweeting, blogging, wiki's, collaborative and co-creative websites etc

I am still convinced today that personal knowledge management is 'the most essential life skill' for the 21st century for the knowledge worker

Team Knowledge Management and Innovation

The next vertical level of the framework represents the team dimension. A number of organizations have implemented a strategy for team knowledge management and innovation. This is an approach that comes from the realization that teams are the key knowledge work units, or knowledge engines, of the organization.

It has been recognized that a team that 'collaborates' well transfers knowledge between members much faster, and, as importantly, is a powerful creator of new knowledge. Project team leaders can now produce new knowledge as a key deliverable, as well as, and alongside, the traditional key project deliverables. Team knowledge management and innovation, therefore, is based on what we call the 'Share' or 'Pull' models of information and knowledge transfer, as opposed to the 'Send' or 'Push' models that are overused and create information overload. But even today, too many team members 'push' information to other team members in email. They become overloaded with information, are highly stressed, and most importantly, lose the overview, and even the meaning and purpose for being a team. Team knowledge management and innovation should be based on team knowledge plans, to proactively define the new knowledge that will be created in each project.

With the introduction of powerful collaborative team technologies, in the late 1980's early 1990's, it became possible, for the first time, for more effective collaborative virtual and cross-functional team working across organizations and across the globe. As with personal knowledge management and innovation, team knowledge management and innovation has been greatly accelerated by mobile, wireless and web-based communication, collaboration and co-creation tools.

At this stage, it should be mentioned that the dimensions of both personal knowledge management and innovation, firstly, and team knowledge management and innovation, secondly, heavily overlap with the notion of the 'Learning Organization' and the need to develop, at a personal level, the five learning disciplines of personal mastery, mental models, shared vision, team learning and systems thinking. This is described in more detail by Peter Senge in his landmark 1990 book, *The Fifth Discipline: The Art and Practice of The Learning Organization*. Importantly, the strategies, methods, tools and techniques used for effective team knowledge management and innovation will be different to the other dimensions.

Organizational Knowledge Management and Innovation

The next vertical level of the framework represents the organizational dimension. Many organizations have first embarked on an 'organizational knowledge management and innovation' approach. The intention being to introduce a strategy and a supporting infrastructure for better creating, storing, sharing and applying knowledge across the entire organization. This approach is primarily a 'top down approach'. It starts by identifying the key knowledge assets, or critical knowledge assets of the organization that are needed to achieve its objectives, and then sets out to develop and leverage those assets to better achieve the organizations' objectives.

To do this, the organization sets up an organization-wide infrastructure and processes to enable the identification, capturing, storing, sharing and applying of knowledge, better knowledge retention, and the re-use of knowledge assets. More continuous and collective processes are implemented, to capture new learning's and ideas before, during, and after work events, and then turn them into good practice and knowledge repositories. Organization-wide expert locators, and communities of practice are also created, to open up and accelerate the flow of knowledge, and to better surface the valuable 'tacit' knowledge that resides in the heads of people, and better uncover valuable knowledge nuggets.

Powerful organizational knowledge systems and tools are used to support these organization-wide knowledge activities, including intranets, knowledge portals, enterprise taxonomies, collaborative work spaces, locators, network and community tools, powerful search, document management systems, wiki's, blogs, tweets, mobile and wireless tools. Once again, the strategies, methods, tools and techniques used for effective organizational knowledge management and innovation, will be different to the other dimensions.

Inter-Organizational Knowledge Management and Innovation

The next vertical level of the framework represents the inter-organizational dimension. This level refers to inter-enterprise relationships and knowledge value networks and partnerships. Hence, knowledge networks with customers, suppliers, partners, competitors, sub-contractors, stakeholders etc.

Some organizations have embarked on these relationships at a global level, for example, inter-governmental agencies, United Nations agencies, regional knowledge networks and knowledge clusters, and the development of common national knowledge platforms etc. Inter-Organizational knowledge management and innovation is based on the realization that the most valuable knowledge sources and resources can be, and probably are, outside your own organization. Very rarely indeed, can an organization have more, and better, knowledge within, compared with the unlimited diversity of rich knowledge that resides without. So commercial organizations and educational establishments are increasingly co-partnering with customers, suppliers and even competitors, to collaborate, co-create, share and develop new knowledge and innovative products and services, together, as one.

Naturally, the global world wide web has enabled a common communications, collaboration, learning, information management, and a knowledge sharing environment. Global mass collaboration initiatives, knowledge systems and knowledge ecologies are now rapidly emerging for the common good. Knowledge Commons for all is an increasing reality. Once again, the strategies, methods, tools and techniques used for effective inter-organizational knowledge management and innovation will be different to the other dimensions.

Global Knowledge Management and Innovation

By now, you may have concluded that there are too many vertical dimensions to consider! But be patient. There is one more important vertical dimension and that is 'Global knowledge management and Innovation'. Actually, to be precise, there are more, at least seven! NASA, since 2003, have been presenting and publishing their 25 year plan for inter-planetary knowledge management and innovation, and quantum physicists are increasingly understanding the power of sub-atomic knowledge management and innovation, but let's stick in this paper to the 5 dimensions of knowledge management and innovation this year, as these are the domains that every business must consider in a highly inter-connected world.

A few organizations have embarked on global knowledge management and innovation initiatives in the past. This is because, initially, this dimension has only been concerned with global organizations. But with the global web, everything has changed dramatically. With the global web, we can very easily become global individuals, global teams and global organizations and communities. It's a radical and fundamental change in our increased potential, productivity, capability and ability to co-create and innovate. In the 1980's the introduction of the personal computer greatly empowered the individual. In the 21st Century, the global web has greatly empowered the global individual, team, organization and community. But again, at the global dimension, the strategies, methods, tools and techniques used for effective global knowledge management and innovation will be different to the other dimensions discussed.

Inter-relationships between the five dimensions of Knowledge and Innovation

As can be seen, from the very brief descriptions above of each of the five dimensions, viewed separately, they are, each, very powerful in their own right. They are completely different in their approach. They tend to have quite different Knowledge and Innovation strategies and can use quite different methods tools and techniques to be successfully implemented. But they are not separate at all! They never ever were! They are all one and the same thing. They are all on the same one spectrum.

They are one knowledge entity made up of individuals! The only thing that is different is the scale of the knowledge entity.

Going back to my earlier concern, we must not put people, who are highly complex organisms, into classical limiting organizational structures and expect them to perform at their best. Importantly, each part, each person, each dimension, is related to each other part, person and dimension, and to the whole. As you improve any part, so you improve all the other parts, and the whole. It is impossible not to do so. Each part is vital to the whole. This results in a virtuous, or upwards spiralling, path of increasing value. More importantly, if any part is missing, it disables the whole from achieving its overall potential and effectiveness. This can even result in a vicious, or downward spiralling path of decreased value.

They are vibrant knowledge ecologies.

If you examine, in more detail, the characteristics of each dimension you will discover that they are all vital to the whole, but no one dimension is complete. Nothing, ultimately, should be omitted. For example, the most common mistake is to embark on organizational knowledge management and innovation, with its espoused organizational benefits, without communicating the individual benefits and personal knowledge management. People, in this case, treat this initiative as yet another organizational initiative and there is no, or very little, motivation, no clear 'what's in it for me', no sustainability. This is doomed to eventual failure because the key knowledge asset is the individual.

As another example, if the organization embarks only on personal knowledge management and innovation, it can only go so far before it reaches its personal limitations in scaling and working across the entire organization and with its stakeholders. This can bring reasonable results, but only mediocre results compared to what is really possible. If an organization embarks only on team knowledge management and innovation, it will miss the extra powerful benefits that personal knowledge management and innovation brings to the team, and the benefits from an enterprise wide organizational knowledge management and innovation infrastructure. It, too, will also only go so far before it reaches its team limitations in scaling and working across the organization and its stakeholders.

If an organization embarks only on inter-organizational knowledge management, without the benefits from personal, team and organizational knowledge management and innovation, it will certainly reach limitations and produce mediocre results.

But effective knowledge management and innovation can and should produce extraordinary results!

Extraordinary knowledge management and innovation results require a strategy that is designed to develop, ultimately, a synthesis from and between, each of the five critical dimensions in the knowledge networking levels. Extraordinary knowledge management and innovation requires a holistic approach.

The sum, the emergent properties from the whole, will be so much greater than the parts! I would positively challenge every organization that is interested in successful, effective, and extraordinary knowledge management and innovation to ask itself if it is applying a holistic approach to all the five dimensions that are discussed in this paper? Is the organization achieving increased value through a virtuous upward spiral of effective knowledge working, creativity, co-creativity and innovation?

I also challenge organizations that seek external help from knowledge management and innovation consultants to ask the consultants to demonstrate the value and benefits that they are gaining as individuals and teams, at least, in their daily lives. If they cannot demonstrate this, then why not? Why are they not benefitting themselves from, at very least, the personal and team dimensions? If they cannot, it means that they do not fully understand the five dimensions of knowledge and innovation. If they cannot, it means that they are not yet fully in the paradigm of effective 21st Century knowledge working in a global knowledge economy.

The Five Emergent Properties of Knowledge and Innovation

You will have noticed that I have only discussed, so far, the five 'vertical' dimensions of knowledge and innovation in the Five Dimension Framework. The five horizontal boxes represent the five key stages, and their 'naturally emergent properties'. In essence, this means that if you apply the right strategies, methods and tools to bring about effective communications and information management, for each of the five dimensions, you will see that people will 'naturally' want to start to coordinate, cooperate and collaborate.

Effective collaboration will 'naturally' lead to increased learning, knowledge transfer, and operational knowledge management.

Effective operational knowledge management will 'naturally' lead to the need for strategic knowledge asset management and this, ultimately, leads 'naturally' to new innovative knowledge creation, co-creation and innovation management. In summary, there are five stages, each with their own emergent properties (higher levels will naturally emerge). So, this holistic implementation framework for knowledge and innovation, can be used to assess where your organization is now, where you would like it to be in, say, 12 months time, and help you to identify and develop the best strategy, methods and tools to enable you to get there in the most effective way. Furthermore, this holistic framework is an invaluable tool to help your organization to identify, better manage, and apply your key strategic and operational knowledge assets. This means that there are five clear bridges between effective communications, collaboration, learning and knowledge management, strategic knowledge asset management and innovation.

In summary, the five vertical and the five horizontal dimensions of the knowledge and innovation framework, and their inter-relationships to form a holistic approach for KM, is critical to success and extraordinary results. Further information about the Strategic Knowledge Asset Management Methodology (KAM) frameworks and tools may be found on our website, or write to me, personally.

ronyoung@knowledge-associates.com

www.knowledge-associates.com

ABOUT THE AUTHOR

Ron Young is the founder of Knowledge Associates International, a knowledge management education, consulting and solutions group with companies based at St Johns Innovation Centre, Cambridge, UK, USA, Japan, Russia and India. He is acknowledged as a leading international expert and thought leader in strategic knowledge asset management and innovation. He specializes in knowledge driven results for organizations. He advised and assisted the UK DTI Innovation Unit in 1999 in the production of the UK Government White Paper 'UK Competitiveness in the Knowledge Driven Economy'.

He regularly provides keynote presentations and workshops at leading knowledge management & innovation conferences around the world. He has chaired for several years both the British Standards Institute (BSI) Knowledge Management Standards Committee and the European Knowledge Management Standards Committee. He is a visiting lecturer/speaker for international business and global knowledge economy programs. He runs accredited Knowledge Asset Management master classes at King's College Cambridge University, UK. He is a consultant for the World Bank, Washington, USA, the European Commission, Joint Research Centre, Brussels, and Asian Productivity Organization, Tokyo, Japan.

He has developed knowledge and innovation strategies and solutions, for major multi-national corporations, international UN agencies, national governments, military, security, and professional institutions around the world. He was a lead consultant for the European Commission 2 Million euro 'Know-Net' Consortium, and 1 million euro LEVER project.

He is joint author of the books 'Knowledge Asset Management' (Springer 2003), 'Upside Down Management' (McGraw Hill Europe 1996), Knowledge Management: Facilitators Guide (Asian Productivity Organization, Tokyo, 2009), Knowledge Management: Case Studies for SME's (APO, Tokyo, 2009), Knowledge Management Tools and Techniques (APO, Tokyo, 2010), Knowledge Management for the Public Sector (APO, Tokyo 2013), APO Demonstration Projects (APO Tokyo, 2015), Knowledge Productivity for the Public Sector (APO, Tokyo, 2017).

BIBLIOGRAPHY

Lorriman, John. & Young, Ron. & Kalinauckas, Paul. (1995). *Upside down management : revolutionizing management and development to maximize business success.* London ; New York : McGraw-Hill Book Co.

Mentzas, G., Apostolou, D., Abecker, A., Young, R. (2003). *Knowledge asset management: Beyond the process-centered and product-centered approaches.* London: Springer.

Senge, P.M., *The fifth discipline : the art and practice of the learning organization.* 1st ed. New York: Doubleday/Currency, 1990.

WHERE IS KM GOING?

ABOUT THE CHAPTER

History is a puzzle comprised of many interrelated pieces often provided by eye witnesses. The nature of each individual's contribution often depends on that person's personal experiences and perspectives, even prejudices. This chapter is one person's own individual perspective on the evolution of knowledge management (KM) from 1995 to the present. Someday, someone will compile a large sampling of such perspectives and viewpoints and we will have a more complete and possibly accurate history of KM's startup.

But, more important at the moment than a history of KM's startup is the question, "Where is KM going?"

Where KM is going will of course be based somewhat on where it's been (its roots), and what technology disruptions are going to shape its ultimate future. e.g., robots, drones and artificial intelligence. Hence, this chapter briefly addresses where KM has been, and then especially focuses on some ideas about where KM is going.

The chapter is in two parts: the first is one perspective on where KM has been, by a person who has been in KM since its very beginnings (1995); and then six different, emerging threads that will no doubt enrich the fabric of future KM.

These threads include: 1) a shift from traditional repositories for content management to much more granular knowledge housed in process-oriented **knowledge bases**; 2) emergence of robust **KM methodologies**, not just ad hoc frameworks and roadmaps; 3) the emergence of **advanced maturity models** as powerful business improvement tools, that are more than just diagnostic assessments, but prescriptive tools as well; 4) attempts to define KM by **competency areas** to enable the development of university curricula and help to establish KM as an actual discipline – diplomas being awarded; 5) increased consideration of KM as not just another improvement discipline, but in fact the instigator and enabler of the requisite major transformation by organizations to operate highly effectively in the next episodic event, the Knowledge Age; and finally, 6) a major shift from KM technology solutions, such as repositories, to a focus on human performance in the Knowledge Age.

This chapter is:

Please cite as:

Weidner, D. (2018). Where is KM going? In J. P. Girard & J. L. Girard (Eds.), *Knowledge management matters: Words of wisdom from leading practitioners* (165-185). Macon, GA: Sagology.

9

WHERE IS KM GOING?

BY DOUGLAS WEIDNER

One Long-Term Knowledge Manager's Perspectives on KM's Roots by Chronological Stages and Future

Mid-to Late 1990s.

Let me tell you a story about KM in the mid- to late-1990s as I experienced it. In 1994, I was a consultant at a U.S. Department of Defense (DoD) think tank focusing on Business Process Reengineering (BPR) and Financial Analysis. DoD is a leader in seeking out ways to improve huge enterprises and it had focused on BPR from the very beginning (about 1992). By 1994, it was determined that despite the potential, DoD's BPR success was mediocre at best. So, DoD commissioned a study group of 30 top consultants from some of the best consulting firms in the Washington, DC area (including a few of the think tanks), to uncover the causative problems and to make specific recommendations.

One of the primary conclusions was that BPR lacked a robust, proven methodology. For instance, most existing BPR methodologies at the time didn't include much about change management or strategic planning. So, we invested much time creating a robust BPR Methodology. At the end of the study, it was determined that the methodology should be published and distributed to all BPR vendors. I was asked to publish the methodology as a representative of a neutral think tank.

The publishing assumption was it should be a typical, hard-copy procedure manual.

But, I had a personal bias against procedure manuals. That's another story, but here it is in a nutshell. I graduated from the U.S. Air Force Academy, where the frequent updates of the Cadet Manual was one amongst many discipline training efforts. Such cadet manuals didn't need many changes, they had been around since West Point (U.S. Army) was founded in 1802. The changes were less on substance than 'probably' just to make sure each cadet learned to be disciplined in all things. I saw through the effort, whether my interpretation was right or not, who knows? But, that experience made me biased against hard copy procedure manuals. So, I started to lobby for an alternative, an electronic procedure manual – obvious today, but quite radical in 1994. The primary argument was: "You can't depend on thousands of admin folks to remove/replace the many changes that would be necessary to continuously enrich the initial manual." Also, think how many trees could be saved.

When the e-manual was completed, it satisfied the Knowledge-Age imperative to 'get the best knowledge to the right person at the right time', which could easily be the KM mantra. But in 1995, KM was definitely and primarily about repositories, and to a lesser extent, expert locators.

Here's why. To be successful a new discipline needed active sales efforts, which could be justified and provided if the result was a multi-million dollar sale. In those days, multi-million dollar sales were possible if the product was the licensing and installation of an enterprise-wide system, i.e., a repository.

Here's a typical late-1990s KM consultant strategy, which continues to the present. Make inroads into an organization on the basis of their potential interest in the "new thing" (KM) and eventual organizational improvement possibilities, which is the chief executive's primary objective.

In truth, in the late 1990s, it would have been almost impossible for a solo KM consultant to survive, unless they could be the spear point to an eventual big system sale (the shaft of the spear). That typically meant being a consultant within an IT consultancy, which is exactly what I was. Truthfully, it was hard for such a consultant to cover their costs with billable hours, so many of us often incurred many overhead hours, which should have been more accurately allocated to marketing expense than overhead. I recall one $325 million NASA contract that was awarded to us, according to the government contracting officer, who essentially said, "Most all proposals documented great capabilities, but only your firm touted KM in response to our request for innovation." I knew my "KM for Rocket Scientists" lectures had helped earn my keep that year.

So, while I saw the power of repositories, I believed process-oriented KBases were the ultimate "KM End Game." But that insight was an overstatement, as many other initiative types were emerging by 2000. It was also pre-mature as the emphasis was clearly on repositories. See more on granular, process-oriented KBases below, #1 in "Where is KM going?"

Back to the late 1990s. KM repositories, could be labeled 'Collect'. More precisely, the collection was explicit documents in a repository. Also, some additional KM methodologies started to emerge, e.g., Amrit Tiwana

Knowledge Management Toolkit, 2000, which could be dubbed *KM* (as a) *System Approach*.

Early 2000s.

By 1999, the US Civilian Government (and many others around the world) were getting very interested in KM, but many were aware of both the mediocre success of 1990s KM, and the growing movement toward the sharing of tacit knowledge (e.g., Expert Locators, CoPs, Knowledge Cafés, etc.) as opposed to a prior focus primarily on explicit information and knowledge. That movement was strong enough that many in the U.S. government even suggested changing the name of KM to *Knowledge Sharing* (KS).

I definitely believed KS was a key KM scope expansion. For instance, in 1999 I coined a label for the KBase while consulting to the United Nations, which I called *Connect & Collect*. Where collect was the KBase content, possibly created by experts. But if that content fell short of an individual's needs, connect was pointers to experts who might assist. Conversely, some KBases might be originally compiled by conversations amongst experts, and if collected, could be the KBase for future practitioners.

So as a member of various government advisory committees, here's what I suggested based on my first-hand knowledge of the KM marketplace. Many software vendors and consultants were committed to KM as a system, and would be reluctant to change that global focus, just because the US government thought KS should pre-empt KM. I also asked, if KM is called KS, what about knowledge creation? Do we ignore the creation of new knowledge in favor of just focusing on existing, sharable knowledge? In my experience, that would ultimately be a big mistake.

The KM name was never changed, but it did indicate a post 2000 transition to much more focus on connect and conversations vs. just documented explicit knowledge. Primarily, I think the future of KM will be less about just traditional KM – a few enterprise systems or techniques, than ultimately about the emerging tools and techniques to gain the advantages of untapped human potential. At the KM Institute, this initiative is called Personal Knowledge Management. Organizations must leverage a new class of high-performing Knowledge Workers as enablers of their requisite organizational transformation, to survive and prosper in the Knowledge Age.

Some additional post-2020 techniques that I see are described below. These predictions are of course based on my own personal KM perspectives, but my confidence in all the below has continue to grow. In the context of "if and when". I am very confident that 'if' is not an issue, just 'when'.

Where is KM going? Summary of Six Predictions.

Though an understanding of where we have been is very helpful, it is more important to answer the question, "Where is KM going?" KM is certainly going to be based on where it's been (its roots), but must be understood in the context of what disruptions are going to shape its ultimate future.

This section is in six diverse parts, which represent a sampling of the many emerging movements that in my considered opinion will define KM by 2020 and beyond, including:

Prediction 1: Performance Support

I predict we will move from repositories as the primary content management source to much more granular knowledge, housed in decision support systems and process-oriented knowledge bases, such as complex processes or methodologies, especially when high turnover is a factor. Such a change will provide 'Performance Support'. It will probably even revolutionize certain types of traditional organizational training, which will involve less classroom training and much more teaching on how to use and leverage KBase Tools and content to gain the best knowledge, but only when needed—aka 'Just-in-Time' learning vs. traditional 'Just-in-Case' learning.

Prediction 2: KM Methodology

I predict we will move from ad-hoc frameworks and roadmaps, suitable for executive briefings and 'calls to action', to very robust KM Methodologies, which will become a requisite for successful KM.

Prediction 3: KM Maturity Models

I predict robust KM Methodologies will enable us to move from ad-hoc maturity models to fact- or evidence-based models that are not just assessment (diagnostic) tools, but will likely become powerful, prescriptive tools for substantial performance improvement as well. And, perhaps unlike performance support, which will take a while to convince folks to think granular, immediately useful knowledge vs. documents, prescriptive maturity models could happen very soon.

Prediction 4: Defined Competency Areas

I predict KM will mature from ill-defined, uncatalogued, and disparate KM efforts to defined KM competency areas. This will enable the development of more standardized university curricula, and for academics to be able to meaningfully organize the many already-proven KM Initiatives into a rich transformative discipline.

Prediction 5: KM as a Transformational Discipline

I predict we will begin to consider KM as not just another improvement discipline (TQM, BPR, etc.), but in fact the instigator and major enabler of the requisite transformation necessary for organizations to operate effectively and be sustainable as viable organizations in the Knowledge Age.

Prediction 6: Human Capital vs. Technology Focus

Finally, I predict major changes in future KM focus, with an increasing migration from technology-focused solutions e.g., the KM Systems Approach described above, to a much-needed focus on increasing human motivations and individual performance in the Knowledge Age. In well-managed K-Age transformations a class of Knowledge Workers will emerge to be highly-motivated and high-performing Personal Knowledge Managers.

Where is KM going? Details of Six Predictions.

Prediction 1: Performance Support

Process-oriented Knowledge Bases vs. Repositories as a "Collect" Tool.

Let me continue the story started in the intro. After my development of a KBase for BPR, I entered the KM fray thinking that KBases might eventually supplant traditional repositories--not for policies, regulations, statutes, and other traditional documents, but certainly for complex processes and methods, especially where turnover was high. I was reinforced in this belief when in 1997 I presented a keynote speech at the American Society for Training and Development. (*Knowledge Management - Concepts and Tools*, National Conference, American Society for Training and Development, May, 1997.) I was preceded by Gloria Gery who was promoting a concept called Performance Support (PS). Performance support evolved from Electronic Performance Support Systems (EPSS), which she wrote about as early as 1989.

She defined Performance Support as "...an integrated electronic environment that is available to and easily accessible by each employee and is structured to provide immediate, individualized on-line access to the full range of information, software, guidance, advice and assistance, data, images, tools, and assessment and monitoring systems to permit job performance with minimal support and intervention by others."

Unfortunately, I don't believe she had progressed much further than a solid concept, and especially gaining the passion to push for that concept against existing interests of the training folks that wanted to avoid any change--especially something as radical as Performance Support. When she saw my presentation, including actual examples of a KBase Tool, that did exactly what she defined as Performance Support, I recall she was ecstatic.

Here's what she saw. See Figures 9-1 and 9-2. Her perspective gave me confidence that I was on the right track, but in KM we had our own vested interests, i.e., the enterprise repository advocates and vendors. But, finally many are beginning to see the need to dig deeper.

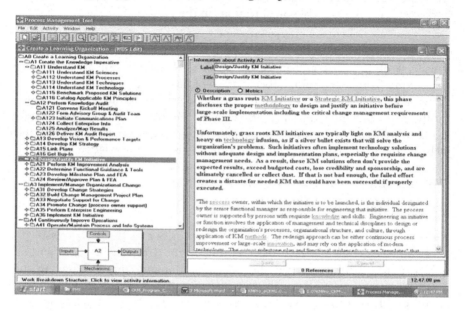

Figure 9-1. Screen shot depicts the original KBase Tool, with initial KM Methodology

This KBase design has three typical components that now seem universal, including an organizing scheme in the left-hand stub, and a description in the right-hand window, as seen in Figure 9-1. For a process-oriented KBase the categorization is typically a work breakdown structure (WBS) or roles. Each WBS activity has a corresponding description.

Obviously, the description is typically an insufficient level of knowledge, so the 'References' button, in the lower, right-hand corner, is typically invoked. It leads to the ultimate knowledge objects or nuggets seen next below (See Figure 9-2Figure).

The critical third key feature includes the actual Knowledge objects themselves, depicted in Figure 9-2, using what I thought to be a creative 'books of knowledge' metaphor. Each book has a particular type of knowledge labeled with both a title and an icon. Icons have emerged to be the more powerful visual approach versus text labels. In 1995, I knew the emerging research, but using clip art icons didn't seem fully adequate, so labels were added as well. The books were constant, but whether they had content varied. Grey scale books were empty.

Every variation of KBases I have seen since 1995 have included these three critical components: an organizing scheme (e.g., WBS or roles); a description of the selected activity; and, the ultimate knowledge nuggets. To be much more helpful, and to fulfill an ultimate KM objective which is to get the best knowledge to the right person at the right time, KBases will become inevitable, the tool that truly enables Performance Support.

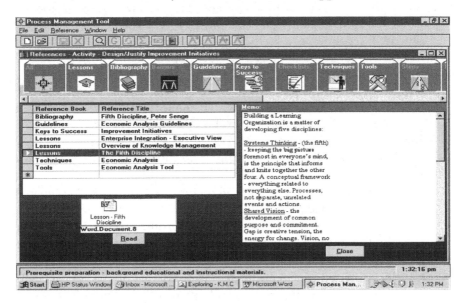

Figure 9-2. Screen shot depicts the functionality of the 1995 version of the KBase Tool

As an aside, I often get criticism today for still using what some think to be an obsolete metaphor – the Books of Knowledge. Metaphors can be very powerful. This one not only anchors the modern Knowledge Age effort to the primary and respected source of historical knowledge down thru the ages (books and libraries), but it focuses on the new Knowledge Age and resultant knowledgebase needs – "get the best knowledge...at the right time", but with a modern digital format delivery, as well.

It further says to me, "The Knowledge Age has been a long time coming, but it is solidly anchored." I like the metaphor and story it relates. You can decide that for yourself, but I think you see the need for much more granular knowledge in the Knowledge Age.

Prediction 2: KM Methodology

I predict we will move from ad-hoc frameworks and graphical roadmaps, certainly suitable for executive briefings and calls to action, but insufficient for detailed implementation guidance, to very robust KM Methodologies, which will become a requisite for successful KM implementations across the globe as KM expands to every nook and cranny.

If you had a robust KM Methodology, it might look like the knowledge base representations in terms of breadth and depth. In addition to understanding the diverse uses of frameworks, roadmaps and especially methodologies, and the need for more evidence-based and robust methodologies, an even more important issue is the biases of today's alternative KM Methodologies. The primary KM methodologies being actually used are what I call "KM (as a) System Approaches." Let's understand why such methodologies are very popular, and why they have had mediocre success.

In my early days as a KM consultant, late 1990s, I was hard pressed to sell enough personal billable hours to justify my employment. Much of my work was to complement information technology presentations with KM briefings.

Such nominal, mostly non-consulting (marketing) efforts resulted in two outcomes.

- A few contracts were won based on our emphasis on KM compared to the more traditional IT consultancies. One such win was a $325 million contract with NASA, where the contracting officer complimented us on our response to their contract requirement for innovative solutions, which of course KM enabled.

- But, more fundamentally, the spear metaphor applied. Specifically, a KM consultant provided a good inroad into a client—the point of the spear. But the consultancy's financial benefit, the shaft of the spear, was the big follow-on IT contract that often followed. So, it is not hard to understand why KM has been very IT oriented, i.e., originally enterprise systems such as repositories. Also, the most successful KM vendors in the early days-and even today, were those focused on enterprise-level systems.

My second KM Methodology prediction is not only that future KM methodologies will become much more rigorous, with proven evidence-based methods, but also the existing bias toward the KM Systems Approach will phase out in favor of a much more transformational KM Methodology. See Prediction #6.

Prediction 3: KM Maturity Models

I predict robust KM Methodologies will enable us to move from ad-hoc, traditional maturity models to evidence-based, predictive models, that are not just typical assessment tools (diagnostics), but will likely be powerful, prescriptive tools as well.

Here's a quick primer on maturity models: They were popularized in the late 1990s by the Software Engineering Institute's – Capability Maturity

Model (CMM)®. The United States government needed a way to pre-screen the hundreds of vendors that would compete on huge IT contracts. Why? Many just weren't qualified, no matter how elegant their proposal, to successfully execute the contract terms. Hence, the CMM® was an assessment focused primarily on consistency of process performance. It became a way to weed out those vendors which had a relatively higher likelihood of failure.

Because of the CMM® popularity, there was a burst of efforts in 1999 to develop a similar Maturity Model for KM. Examples: KM Maturity Model (KMMM)® by Siemens AG, KM Landscape by Microsoft, and my Knowledge Maturity Model (KMM)™, now an asset of the KM Institute. Quite frankly, most of the early maturity models were weak examples of what might be possible if the basis for each assessment was evidence-based vs. ad hoc.

But, in addition, consider going to the doctor's office to get a checkup. What if the doctor said here's what's wrong with you (diagnosis). Come back and see me next year. Would you be satisfied to have a diagnosis with no curative prescription? Probably not. Then why would we assess our own organizations if we couldn't simultaneously provide a prescription for renewed or continued good health?

By 2010, I believed we needed a tool that wasn't just an assessment (diagnostic), but could be enriched by the KM Methodology to provide a prescription as well (see Figure 9-3). Importantly, it doesn't merely address the health of KM, but other threads critical to overall health and prosperity that can be improved through KM and other evidence-based prescriptions.

Figure 9-3. KM Transformation Solution™

It is not obvious from the spiral graphic-like roadmap, but there are a number of actionable threads being evaluated. For each thread at each level, one or more questions are asked. The answers are on a five-point Likert scale.

The multiple threads are determined by deciding on the most critical concerns of the organization under study. Barring such specific knowledge, the most important concerns for all organizations are in the generic model, which include: human capital, customer satisfaction, innovation, analytics, KM and transformational change management.

Obviously, without a robust KM Methodology, the high-level prescription couldn't be parsed into the many diverse recommended activities, such as: for human resources (HR), to get alignment and buy-in from HR; specifically to define ways to substantially improve engagement, develop a relevant KM training curricula, and the specific details on how to implement a Personal Knowledge Manager (PKM)™ certification strategy to improve personal performance in the Knowledge Age.

Prediction 4: Defined KM Competency Areas

I predict KM will mature from ill-defined, uncatalogued, and disparate KM efforts to defined KM competency areas. This will enable the development of university curricula, and a way to begin to meaningfully organize the many already-proven KM Initiatives into a viable discipline.

Many universities around the world have attempted to establish KM departments since the late 1990s. Many have, in my opinion, faltered for a number of reasons, including: 1) low numbers of potential students in the early years; 2) lack of instructors with diverse KM experience; and, 3) weak programs, certainly not of the rigor of established disciplines such as traditional MBAs might teach.

The noticeable press for better university programs started in about 2010, when the KM Education Forum (KMEF) was established by Kent State's KM Program, headed by Dr. Denise Bedford, now at Georgetown University, and by George Washington University (Washington DC), which was represented by Dr. Annie Green.

The goals were traditional for universities and the KM Institute; namely, to first define KM Team Roles, which included Knowledge Managers, Specialists and Practitioners, and Knowledge Workers, as well. Then, to define the skills and competencies required to perform those roles in the Knowledge Age. Once having defined roles and skills, competency areas follow and enable universities to create courses toward recognized diplomas, and for training firms to create training programs to enable rigorous and applicable certifications at various levels.

Here are the Competency Areas that derived from much work by leading universities seeking to establish their own KM programs, and as customized by the KM Institute for its certification programs.

1. **KM410 Series: Transformational Leadership & Strategy.** Transformational Leadership & Strategy is about: KM Frameworks, Roadmaps, KM Methodologies, Governance, Modern Maturity Models, and especially the KM Transformational Solutions, and more. *Enterprise Innovation* – This is a major transformation leadership sub-competency area. It includes tactical and enterprise continuous improvement methods, culture, and technology as well.

2. **KM420 Series: Knowledge Assessment & Evaluation.** Knowledge Assessment & Evaluation is about: Audits, Evidence-Based Analytics, KM Metrics, and more. Also, this area should comply with emerging standards for ISO 9001:2015 - standards for K Audits.

3. **KM430 Series: Culture & Communications.** Culture & Communications is about: Traditional Change Management (e.g., Awareness Campaign: Communication Plan & Learning Plan), Personal Knowledge Management (PKMgmt), and more. Also, this area should comply with emerging standards for ISO 9001:2015 - standards for Cultural Change Mgmt.

4. **KM440 Series: Collaboration & Communities.** Collaboration and Communities is about: K Sharing methods and optimization of social media tools such as: Expert Locators, Communities of Practice (CoPs), Social Network Analysis (SNA), and more. Also, this area should comply with emerging standards for **ISO 9001:2015** - standards for K use and sharing to achieve objectives.

5. **KM450 Series: Knowledge Asset Management.** Knowledge Asset Management is about: explicit knowledge - Knowledge Repositories, Taxonomy, Search, and more. See also KM495 Series: Knowledge Architecture. Also, this area should comply with emerging standards for ISO 9001:2015 - standards for K asset management.

6. **KM460 Series: Intellectual Capital Management.** Intellectual Capital Management is about: tacit K Capture, K Transfer and Retention, and more. Also, this area should comply with emerging standards for ISO 9001:2015 - standards for undocumented K capture and sharing.

7. **KM470 Series: Organizational Learning.** Organizational Learning is about: Performance Support, Rethink Learning (methods & technologies), and more. Also, this area should comply with emerging standards for ISO 9001:2015 - standards for undocumented K capture and sharing.

8. **KM480 Series: K-Embedded Business Operations.** K-Embedded Business Operations is about functional KM initiatives rather than primarily enterprisewide ones. Specifically, it is about: Lessons

Learned and Best Practice Management Processes, Customer Satisfaction, Process Management in the K Age ("Connect & Collect"), and more. Also, this area should comply with emerging standards for ISO 9001:2015 - improved project and process K use and sharing.

9. **KM490 Series: Knowledge Technologies**. Knowledge Technologies is about: Hard Disciplines – Build Apps, Deliver Technology Solutions, and more.

10. **KM495 Series: Knowledge Architecture**. Knowledge Architecture is about: Soft Disciplines – Info Architecture, People-centric Design Solutions, and more.

For a more detailed description of each Competency Area, see our website: www.kminstitute.org

I predict the KM industry will become much better organized, essentially becoming a discipline in the traditional, academic sense – actual KM degree programs in many universities and certification programs from proven commercial trainers. But, to become a respected discipline, KM will need robust methodologies and many more documented successes. In addition, in my opinion, KM will need to morph from a traditional discipline to a transformative one (#5 below), and from a technology focus to a clear emphasis on human capital (#6 below)..

Prediction 5: KM as a Transformational Discipline

I predict we will begin to consider KM as not just another improvement discipline (TQM, BPR, Agile, etc.), but in fact the major enabler of the requisite transformation necessary to operate effectively, and to be sustainable as a viable organization in what will be a very competitive, global Knowledge Age.

When I first started thinking of KM as transformative vs. just a discipline – early 2000s, I got major pushback. The resistance was particularly strident and understandably so, since many KMers were mostly fascinated with KM technology. I was downplaying technology by that time, as being closer to a commodity than the disruptive technologies and methods such as KM itself.

But, experienced change management experts who thought their discipline could cover all types of changes, found the transformative change management approach to be foreign to them. Ironically, many change experts were fearful of the transformative change emphasis, or arrogant--especially about its implications for their traditional change management discipline. Here is an occasional challenge I get in KM Certification Program workshops, "I'm already a certified Change Manager. Your KM Certification touts much about change management, but what can you possibly teach me that I don't already know?" Here's the answer.

Transformational Change Management (TCM) – There are many major differences between traditional CM and transformational CM. Some might consider this an oversimplification, but the section below details the major differences between the two, of which there are many.

Traditional Change Management has a number of primary activities – five primary ones according to a Prosci study in 2011 - *Which CM levers do practitioners typically use?* (Prosci is an established change management trainer.) The primary activities include a Communications Plan (88%) and a Training Plan (76%). Sometimes both are combined and logically dubbed an 'Awareness Campaign'. Three other activities were only minor, in the 10 – 26% range of usage.

Consider how a traditional change management program might be launched for a typical KM technology solution – perhaps a portal-type repository or other enterprise-level system, maybe social media that supports communities of practice and an expert locator.

- **Traditional Communications Plan** – Once the portal was decided upon, the CM Team would start the design of a communications plan. The plan might be implemented either immediately, or closer to the actual system installation, depending on the timing gap between CM kickoff and planned implementation date. Communication initiatives can vary widely and may include announcement speeches often done by key executives, and other announcements such as Newsletters and always updates, etc., but does not include formal training.

- **Traditional (Formal) Training Plan** – Today, it is more typically called a Learning Plan, but the details are the same and quite obvious. The Learning Plan focuses on getting the folks who will be using the new system well trained before implementation. Timing is obviously a key issue as is adequate competence on the new system.

Transformational Change Management is probably best defined in John Kotter's series of books on change, which he started writing in the 1990s. (See source list of Kotter's books at the end of this chapter.)

- **Transformational Communications Plan** – The key communication differences compared to the traditional CM are in the critical need for much actual and personal top management involvement. The KM Team, in conjunction and coordination with top management must create a communications plan that includes at least the following much more demanding needs than traditional CM. Specifically, these additional activities include: a motivating 'Call to Action'; the need to create a 'Sense of Urgency' to accelerate

179

action, and a "clear, compelling vision" as specific guidance; and finally, how to overcome resistors, often called 'Get Buy In'.

- **Transformational Learning Plan** – In addition to specific training related to any early KM Initiatives, Transformational CM requires much more extensive training to educate all employees on the major disruptions being faced by our economy, how to overcome organizational complacency, and the desirability and feasibility of the new Knowledge-Age vision. In addition, I predict a whole class of certification courses focused on making marginally engaged knowledge workers into fully engaged, high-performing Personal Knowledge Managers (PKM)™. This human capital prediction is covered next.

Prediction 6: Human Capital vs. Technology Focus

Finally, I predict major changes in KM focus, with an increasing migration from primarily technology-focused solutions, e.g., the KM Systems Approach as a methodology described above, to a much-needed focus on increasing human motivations and performance in the Knowledge Age. Humans will become the ultimate center of gravity for KM going forward, not technology. The gap between existing technology capability and what is essential to KM is small, compared to the gap between existing human performance and ultimate human potential in the Knowledge Age. (See source list on the whole host of diverse personal knowledge management books at the end of this chapter.)

There has been much, very convincing research, insights and conclusions in the last twenty years by the Gallup Organization and others. This branch of human capital research focuses on human engagement on the job. In general, humans across all job categories and nationalities around the world are only marginally engaged on the job. Typical results are max 25 – 30% engaged. Organizations with much higher levels of engagement inevitably beat the competition.

Fortunately, the Gallup organization not only uncovered very elegant ways to determine average engagement levels in an organization--an assessment tool of just twelve questions, but those questions have potentially, reasonably prescriptive outcomes as well. The Gallup human capital research diagnostic and prescriptive insights and guidance has been incorporated into the Knowledge Maturity Model (KMM)™ described in #3 above.

Conclusion

Six bold predictions have been made and justified. Here they are in summary:

1) There will no doubt be an eventual shift from traditional repositories for content management to much more granular knowledge, housed in

process-oriented **knowledge bases (KBases)**. That is, unless artificial intelligence accelerates rapidly and is applied to this ubiquitous KM need – to get the best knowledge to the right person at the right time. I see a compelling requirement right now, proven by call center operations and the rapid automation of all manner of decision support systems. KBases are best for tightly-defined applications, typically with one or more of these characteristics: complex or dynamic processes or those with high turnover..

2) More robust **KM methodologies** will soon emerge. They will replace the ad hoc frameworks and roadmaps that are insufficient for complex methodologies and process methods. KBases (with KM methodologies) will substantially improve KM performance, as well as the performance of all types of complex processes (process KBases), especially those with high turnover and steep learning curves, and especially those processes that need quick access to in-depth knowledge to help make decisions or solve problems.

3) The next generation of **diagnostic and prescriptive maturity models,** already available, will soon gain a foothold as powerful, evidence-based business improvement tools.

4) **Competency Area** definitions (including scope of roles and associated learning objectives) of KM will soon reach a reasonable consensus. This will accelerate university course and program creation toward KM, especially an MBA in KM. The role of Chief Knowledge Officer (CKO), especially if leading an organizational transformation, cries out for a rigorous MBA in KM.

But, such programs must be at a reasonable, cost-justified price and have above average convenience, considering the concurrent workload of a CKO. Most traditional universities will have trouble with the traditional marketplace, including price competition, product offering and convenience.

Considering my personal experiences, perspectives, and even potential prejudices, I somewhat cautiously predict there will soon be a major disruption in the academic marketplace in general and in KM programs in particular.

A unique MBA in KM may be amongst the first disruptors as the Master CKM certification (**MCKM**) converges on and even overlaps the ideas, philosophies and content of the traditional MBA. Except certification programs have one major competitive advantage for practitioners – a major focus on being able to do, not just to understand. Keep an eye on the KM academic community, and about to be disrupted academic marketplace.

5) KM as not just another improvement discipline, it is the natural response to the current episodic shift in human occupations, which itself is prompted by substantial automation potential of most all means of menial, repetitive work in all quarters. Today, this is no longer speculative. General purpose robots operate at lower per hour costs than cheap Chinese labor. So,

consider--are future factories going to be built in regions with just low-cost labor, or are a new class of Knowledge-Age executives, with transformational intentions, going to seek regions with both an educated and highly motivated work force--that can leverage low-cost computers and production and delivery innovations (make and move) to be price and quality competitive anywhere?

and finally,

6)   For historic, developed-country lifestyles and wealth creation to survive well into the 21st century, humans must focus on the well-documented gap in human performance--between past performance and actual human potential. High-performance humans, partnered with robots, drones and artificial intelligence (AI), will be more than competitive with production anywhere. This might very well be the future of innovation.

Welcome to the Knowledge Age!

I hope my personal perspective on the history of KM, and my six KM predictions, will help you navigate successfully the Knowledge Age, especially including the proven objectives of substantially improved human and organizational performance.

ABOUT THE AUTHOR

Douglas Weidner is a U.S. Air Force Academy graduate and past combat pilot. He has an MBA in Business Economics and an MS in Operations Research. He's been a consultant in diverse, analytical fields: Operations Research, Financial Analysis, Strategic Planning, Total Quality Management (TQM), Business Process Re-engineering (BPR), and change management.

He has been fully involved in KM since its proverbial beginning, when as a US Department of Defense (DoD) think tank consultant (1994), he designed a "Knowledge Base Tool" (KBase), which ultimately housed DoD's BPR Methodology in 1995-6.

About then, KM began to appear over the horizon; hence our KM Institute (KMI) logo.

He almost immediately recognized the major episodic event that was emerging. Convinced that KM was to have a major impact on all human occupations, as did the transformations to the Agrarian, Industrial and Information Ages; he started to consult full time in this new discipline.

In 1995 he actually had a real KM job and title as Chief Knowledge Engineer. His initial consulting was primarily for DoD, including creating an early KM Methodology--housed on the DoD's KBase Tool. Subsequently, he consulted for many of the large and earliest KM initiators – DoD (1995 – 2001), various U.S. Government Agencies, the World Bank 1995 and UN 1999. He trained/consulted for other global organizations, including: Islamic Development Bank, African Development Bank, Aramco and most international petroleum companies, US-AID and many others (2001 – 2017).

But more than those consulting and training activities, which certainly shaped his early KM perspectives, he claims he learned more about KM from teaching and researching for about 10,000 certificants, primarily Certified Knowledge Managers (CKMs) in all types of organizations, starting in 2001.

He founded KMI to do KM certification training; it is now the dominant global provider for all core KM Team roles, especially the Certified Knowledge Manager (CKM), Specialists (CKSs) and Practitioners (CKPs) and for Knowledge Workers as Personal Knowledge Managers (PKM)™.

He serves now as KMI's Executive Chairman; as Chief CKM Instructor he launched the KMI's Train-the-Trainer Program to establish a global network of local CKM Trainers/consulting partners.

Also, he just established the KMI Press™ to provide expanded publishing ability to all KM experts--affordable KM books and the KM Institute's KM Body of Knowledge (**KMBOK**)™. In 2018, he will author and edit the **"Knowledge-Age Transformation Series**. It will include many diverse transformational and futuristic KM topics, such as those predicted in this chapter. Douglas can be contacted at douglas.weidner@kminstitute.org, or through the KM Institute at www.kminstitute.org.

RECOMENDED RESOURCES

Recommended Transformational Change Management Books

All by John Kotter: on Transformational Change Management, especially "A Force for Change", "Leading Change", "A Sense of Urgency", "Buy-In", and "Accelerate" 1990-2014.

All by Malcolm Gladwell: "Tipping Point-How Little Things Can Make Big Difference", "Outliers", "Blink", "David" 2000-2012.

All by Peter Drucker: "Post-Capitalist Society", "Knowledge Management for 21st Century", 1993, 1998 and many others.

All by Clayton Christensen, "Disrupting Class – How Disruptive Innovation Will Change the Way the World Learns," 2008 and many others.

"DIY-U – Coming Transformation of Higher Education," Anya Kamenetz, 2010

"Learning to Fly," Collison & Parcell, 2001, 2004

"Thinking for a Living: How to Get Better Performances and Results from K Workers," T. Davenport, 2005.

"The Wisdom of Crowds – Why the Many are Smarter than the Few and How Collective Wisdom Shapes Business, Economies, Societies, and Nations," by James Surowiecki, 2004.

Recommended Personal KM (PKM)™ Books – Know Yourself.

Malcolm Gladwell: "David and Goliath: Underdogs, Misfits, and the Art of Battling Giants," 2013. See also: "Tipping Point", 2000, "Blink" 2005, "Outliers" 2008, and "What the Dog Saw" 2009.

"Quiet – The Power of Introverts in a World that Can't Stop Talking," Susan Cain, 2013.

"The 7 Hidden Reasons Employees Leave – How to recognize the Subtle Signs and Act Before it's too Late," Leigh Branham, 2012.

"Thinking Fast and Slow," Daniel Kahneman, 2011.

Marcus Buckingham: "First, Break All the Rules: What the World's Greatest Managers Do Differently," 1999. "Now, Discover Your Strengths," 2001. "The One Thing You Need to Know…About Great Managing, Great Leading, and Sustained Individual Success," 2005. "Go put your Strengths to Work," 2007.

Daniel Pink: "Drive – Surprising Truth about what Motivates Us", 2009. "A Whole New Mind – Why Right-Brainers Will Rule Future," 2006.

"Mindset – The New Psychology of Success – Why attitude is as important as talent," Dr. Carol Dweck, 2006.

"Stumbling on Happiness," Daniel Gilbert, 2005.

Stephen Covey: "7 Habits of Highly Effective People: Powerful Lessons in Personal Change," 2004. "8th Habit: Effectiveness to Greatness," 2004.

Martin E. P. Seligman: "Authentic Happiness: Using the New Positive Psychology to Realize Your Potential for Lasting Fulfillment," 2002. "Learned Optimism: How to Change Your Mind and Your Life," 1998.

"How People Learn – Brain, Mind, Experience, and School," National Research Council, 2000.

"Why We Do What We Do – Understanding Self-Motivation," by Edward Deci, 1995.

"Flow: The Psychology of Optimal Experience," by Mi Csikszentmihalyi, 1990.

Daniel G Amen, M.D., "Making a Good Brain Great," 2005. "Magnificent Mind at any Age," 2008. "Change Your Brain, Change Your Body,"2010.

If we wonder often, the gift of knowledge will come.

~ **Arapaho Proverb**

LEADING KNOWLEDGE FLOWS AND COCREATION FOR SUSTAINED FUTURE OUTCOMES

ABOUT THE CHAPTER

This chapter takes a slightly different direction to shift mindsets towards the future of knowledge. We explore how organizations can achieve knowledge flows to drive creativity, innovation and overall performance in what becomes an ongoing learning process to sustain success. Resilience, adaptability and sustainability (business growth and continuity) come from leveraging existing and past knowledge to inform strategy creation, rather than reacting to strategy made in isolation of present knowledge. Leading knowledge initiatives to facilitate a continual flow of knowledge in iterative planning and implementation cycles co-creates new knowledge. This informs the next decision cycle, thereby ensuring learning before, during and ongoing to sustain continuous value growth.

This thinking extends the ideas, concepts and success stories shared in KNOWledge SUCCESSion released in early 2017. However, to provide some basic context, KNOWledge SUCCESSion is a social mindset and approach to how to interact with each other, acknowledging this significantly impacts our success. To KNOW SUCCESS in a sustainable manner, individuals, teams and organizations need to actively manage their KNOWledge SUCCESSion. That is understanding what we need to know, how we come to know it, when we need it and what we need to unlearn or adapt for future application. In principle, KNOWledge SUCCESSion is a strategy for achieving optimal performance in a world of emergent complexity. More than just capture or transfer of knowledge, it combines many interdependent aspects of knowledge to co-create synergies and not just align actions with overall organizational strategy, but to inform strategy creation.

Acknowledgement: This chapter is the output of many conversations with many knowledgeable people over three decades of knowledge work. Too many to individually list here, they include all the authors in this book and many others referenced and not. We are as powerful and knowledgeable as our entire network, IF we choose to connect and build trusted relationships. As knowledge professionals, the sooner we connect the knowledge profession better than we currently do, the better off we will all be and the greater the influence we will have for humanity.

This chapter is:

Please cite as:

Shelley, A. (2018). Leading knowledge flows and cocreation for sustained future outcomes. In J. P. Girard & J. L. Girard (Eds.), *Knowledge management matters: Words of wisdom from leading practitioners* (187-201). Macon, GA: Sagology.

10

LEADING KNOWLEDGE FLOWS AND COCREATION FOR SUSTAINED FUTURE OUTCOMES

BY ARTHUR SHELLEY

It is not possible to:
LISTEN with your mouth open
LEARN with your mind closed
LEAD with a dispassionate heart

The future is being co-created as you read this document - in your own mind, in others' minds and through interactions between connected people. Listening and learning (with and from others) through social interactions, enables us to lead strategically and generate new knowledge. Knowledge is the fuel of the future. In fact, this document is a co-created asset in itself, drawn from the knowledge of several experienced practitioners. Guided and engaged by the leadership of John and JoAnn, a community of like-minded and respected knowledge professionals, collaborated virtually to bring together this book. Of course, this book is not knowledge *per se*, it is information with potential based on knowledge. As you read the insights here, you will create new knowledge as you interpret possibilities to apply them to create value in your own contexts. We will explore how this journey works in practice through this chapter and relate it to the other pieces of the knowledge puzzle contained elsewhere in the book.

The simple structure of the following three reflective questions is very powerful and will be followed in this chapter to provide a practical guide to achieving knowledge management success:

- What?
- So What?
- Now What?

This simple structure provides a highly practical framework for creating and prioritizing strategy, building a roadmap for aligning your knowledge program and implementing the knowledge initiatives. When this is done as proactive iterative cycles to inform organizational strategy (rather than react to it), performance improves.

WHAT? Deciding what creates MOST value is critical to success.

The future is dominated by those who most effectively create and apply their knowledge to achieve the tangible outputs and intangible outcomes they desire.

How can you ever make a good decision without knowledge?

The future is dominated by those who most effectively create and apply their knowledge to achieve the tangible outputs and intangible outcomes they desire. When organizations relax to rest on their past knowledge and performance, they are overtaken by those who continue to accelerate the creation and application of new knowledge. Peter Drucker famously stated, "If you want to predict the future, create it", although there seems to be several other people who have made very similar statements, including attributions to Abraham Lincoln, Ilya Prigogine, Alan Kay, Steven Lisberger, Forrest C. Shaklee and Dennis Gabor a Nobel prize winner (O'Toole, 2016). The point I make here is, we are often unsure where an idea comes from and who else has adapted it, or even independently created the same idea in parallel. What we do know, is that such insights can become useful in a future situation to help inform and influence our thinking as well as others. What we know (are able to recall) is okay for games of trivia. However, far more important is how can we apply, adapt and combine this with other ideas in the present to create value, or sustain future value creation.

When ideas are bounced between people through conversation, they recombine, multiply and evolve to create new knowledge that did not exist previously. This is what drives creativity, which is the precursor of innovation (given the right culture, behaviour, intent and resources). Leveraging a diversity of perspectives around an idea or concept, enables those involved in the interaction (usually a conversation, but also activities like games, improvisation, simulations and projects) to each bring adaptation to the knowledge that is being created. If this is done in an environment of open mindset and mutual respect, it rapidly generates a wide range of options to progress the potential into greater possibilities.

There are ways to design visualization activities to enhance the process of co-creation of new knowledge and also to connect ideas that are not intuitively related. In his book, *Seeing What Others Don't*, Gary Klein described three ways that the insight generation can be stimulated. Figure 10-1 summarizes these ideas and the environment around them that is essential to the flow of knowledge.

Klein stated that insights can come from Contradictions, Connections or Creative Desperation. Each of these require reflection in order to consciously realise the insight. This reflection is accelerated when people can explore the possibilities with each other. Often the inclusion of a comment from a slightly different angle or perspective is sufficient for the apparent eureka moment to be generated.

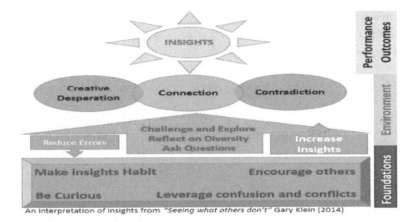

Figure 10-1. Insights about sources of insights

This idea of a creative mix of many elements fermenting to percolate into a new brew of ideas, knowledge and concepts things was also discussed by Eric Weiner in *The Geography of Genius*. His research highlighted the common elements of a co-creative environment to optimize knowledge creation and innovation:

- Mentors and Sponsors
- Freshness – openness to new ideas and emergence
- Chaos and disorder to challenge patterns and motivate to act
- Diversity and openness to ideas shared in a trusted environment encouraging boundaries to be crossed
- Discernment driving competitive tension
- "Genius Clusters" – communities of practice engaged in diversity of ideas and social conversations

- Place – a sense of belonging with a location that has a culture of appreciation that attracts wealth and talent to create value

A key understanding from this train of thought is that the knowledge is just the foundation of what needs attention. Yes, Knowledge IS critical. However, it is NOT the focus. Knowledge is the fuel of success on our journey, not the journey itself. It optimizes value creation when its flow is accelerated to inform decision making and drive innovation. An alternative metaphor is knowledge is water. Both knowledge and water generate power when flowing, but only offers potential when stagnant. Too many knowledge management programs are limited in the value they create, because they focus on the capture and storage of the knowledge and not on the value it will create when applied.

The idea that knowledge is a critical foundation is not new. Benjamin Bloom's seminal work on learning highlighted that knowledge, interpreted as the ability for people to remember ideas and concepts, was the foundation of learning. Like modern KM programs, his criticism was too much teaching practice was focused on the remembering aspects, and not enough on the higher orders of learning as shown in Figure 10-2.

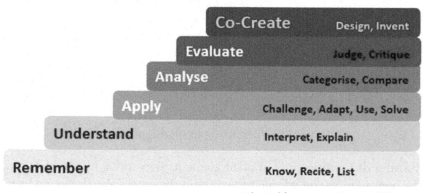

Adapted from original work of Bloom

Figure 10-2. An adapted action version of the hierarchy of learning

Figure 10-2 highlights that the success of your knowledge initiative is that success comes from leveraging this knowledge as the foundation of knowing, through the levels of the hierarchy to the ultimate state of being able to co-create new knowledge, products and services or increasing capabilities and productivity through the flow of knowledge through these levels. Notice the flow in this form has been converted to verbs, to highlight it is through actions that this conversation takes place. We start by knowing (possession of knowledge) to elevate our understanding so that we can apply, then analyse and make judgements about the quality of that knowledge (and highlight the gaps we have in our knowledge). This gets us to WHAT we know and what we don't know. With such depth of insights we can explore what the implications of our situation is to achieve a strong sense of SO WHAT. This creates a foundation for optimal decision making around NOW WHAT, that is, strategizing the optimal way forward. Discussions about now what, can't be as successful without consideration of the knowledge of the earlier reflections and this is where many strategic conversations lose their way.

Often those creating strategy are in the uppermost levels of the hierarchy, making them somewhat remote from the current business operations, both in physical distance and in their level of current operational knowledge. Figure 10-3 highlights that the creation of new knowledge at a practical level is happening at the "coal face" of the organization's operations, not at the upper levels. The longer leaders have been distanced from the current actions the more they make assumptions about what is actually happening. This is largely because their knowledge is based on what happened when they were there, and not on current practice. This detachment from the operations can be a positive as it allows them to take a bigger picture view of the organization. However, it can also be a limitation as many aspects of the operations have moved on (hopefully in a positive way through incremental or even disruptive improvements).

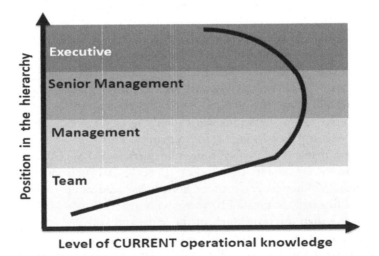

Figure 10-3. The distribution of current knowledge in organizations

The challenge for senior leaders to avoid is make strategic decisions in the absence of current knowledge, thereby generating a suboptimal strategy. Creating a cycle of new knowledge flow up to the strategy creators to ensure they are able to take advantage of ongoing learning, enables prioritization of optimal and sustainable next steps. The challenge with this is it is a reversal of how many organizational leaders view the direction of communications. Many modern businesses work on a downward cascade of strategic communications once the decisions have been made and expect the lower levels in the hierarchy to react to the directions being dictated.

It is important to include the new knowledge and learning from the previous cycles and levels as we formulate a strategic approach to our longer term goals and then define a way to deliver on that through a detailed execution plan. Including both existing and new knowledge in these iterative cycles (as well as considering yet to be generated possible knowledge) enables us to optimally inform strategy creation, rather than react to it.

There are many exploratory tools that enable inclusive conversations about WHAT we have, and what we can do next to elevate understanding. Some of these are described in *Being A Successful Knowledge Leader* (Shelley, 2009) and others in *KNOWledge SUCCESSION* (Shelley, 2017)

SO WHAT? Understanding implications of your actions matters

The short answer to "so what" is that humanity is not leveraging its collective knowledge as effectively as it could. There are many errors being repeated around the world, with major tangible and intangible losses. More projects fail to meet their objectives than are successful and this is often a result of not deploying the right knowledge in the right way for their context. With strategic, collective, proactive approaches to knowledge development and deployment, we can reduce costs and innovate faster. Directly connecting iterative co-creative approaches to knowledge development and better aligning knowledge initiatives with organizational strategies, will make major contributions to productivity and social value creation. The social capital that will be created from the actions listed below will make a significant contribution to how we better manage everything we do as individuals, teams, organizations - and dare I suggest, for humanity.

There are many good quality, longer answers to SO WHAT. These can be summarized by a shift in mindset (Dweck, 2016), from a focus on management of knowledge to more knowledge leadership (Shelley, 2009, 2017). The future is co-created by those who generate new knowledge and apply it faster than the rest. Much of the skills and knowledge of people in traditional roles is rapidly being replaced by AI (Artificial Intelligence), which has huge social implications for the millions of people in routine roles. This shift in our economies is not a future prediction, it is already happening in many task-based jobs (Frank, Roehrig and Pring, 2017). The future of the knowledge profession will be increasingly focused on the generation of new insights and decreasingly interpreting what we can learn from the past. I am not suggesting that it is past OR present OR future. It is learning from the past to make better decisions in the present to create a range of superior future options. Our paradigm is not a dichotomous either or, is it one of multiple ANDS. This and that, and that and that too. Not this OR that. Our present complex environment is already multidimensional with many parallel "truths" and this is going to become increasingly complex as new technology and social interactions drive even more rapid emergent change.

The implications of this, is success will come from being more comfortable in uncertainty and being able to act in emergent ways. That is, build in the confidence and ability to act faster with the understanding that not all required knowledge is available at the time decisions are taken. However, also have the confidence that the knowledge gaps cannot be filled without acting. The act of doing something – a calculated best guess - is better than not doing anything, because the new knowledge only emerges when the actions are taken. Our role as knowledge leaders is to be a role model for other knowledge professionals to build their capabilities to become the next generation of leaders (Snowden, 2007, Bennet et al 2017).

NOW WHAT? Co-creating and prioritizing what happens next

Too often people spend too much time on What and So What, and don't progress the conversation to Now What. The first two conversations help us to understand the past and present, but do little to invoke actions to make a better future. In order to make a difference for ourselves, our teams and beyond, we need to act on what we have come to know through reflecting in the prior two questions and the implications these may bring.

What we need to be evolving towards is balanced ecosystems in which the elements of the system operate in harmony through good communications throughout. However, in modern complex organizations, power and money games get politicized and personalities and ambitions tend to focus on short term tactics over long term strategies. Rather than harmonized ecosystems we get unsustainable *egosystems* where interpersonal conflicts get in the way of high quality decisions and ultimately the flow of knowledge. This is why so many organizations underperform and make so many errors. These challenges increase employee turnover, thereby exacerbating knowledge losses. There are five BIG opportunities to advance the direction and impact that knowledge can have to making a better world. In collectively taking these steps, we will co-create a new identity we will come to belong to which is the *International Knowledge Professional Society*.

The first BIG now what opportunity is optimizing knowledge flow. This depends on senior managers and leaders engaging with lower level managers operating at the coal face, to listen to their insights and understand the practical challenges the organization faces. It also requires managers to listen to the vision and direction the leaders are trying to achieve and discuss with them how they can remove these barriers to enable higher performance. Unfortunately, too few organizations engage in proactive, open-minded dialogue enough. Where it does work, there are active communities of practice exchanging ideas on improvements and these ideas are formulated into possible projects. The leaders of the communities have a trusted advisor relationship (Maister and Green, 2000) with the upper levels, who engage with them in "Conversations That Matter" (Shelley, 2009) to prioritize the highest strategic value options. These options then become the foundation of the next strategic cycle to deliver the future performance.

The second now what opportunity is the realization that knowledge initiatives play a critical role in these strategic dialogues. Too often the knowledge teams are relatively junior roles in the organization and largely reactive to the strategy or worse, focused on IT or knowledge capture projects. When knowledge roles are recognized higher in the organization and filled with people of greater experience, more impact is made on organizational performance. This is partially because more senior people are more widely connected and influential, but also because when people of such levels and capabilities understand how the application of knowledge stimulates performance, they allocate more funds to invest in supporting knowledge initiatives. This in turn accelerates what can be achieved and multiplies value generation.

The third now what opportunity is to shift mindsets though four stages of understanding and capability (Shelley, 2017). Awareness is the foundation, followed by Attitude, then Ability and finally Action. The order of these stages of mindset adjustments is important. By explaining why knowledge initiatives create value, we create awareness. This is a mindset shift from "why?" to "I understand why". A shift from a question in non-understanding to one of knowledge. Once the target stakeholder understands why, you then work with them to build a supportive attitude. Change is usually met by resistance and this can be changed to support by engaging the right behaviours and highlighting the impacts the new way forward will generate benefits for them. With awareness and a more positive attitude, it is important to then address ability. That is, competency and confidence by training the stakeholders to take action. This cycle of development of the mindset through these stages works well. However, if one simply demands action without explaining why (awareness), you certainly get attitude! (and not the supportive type one needs to accelerate knowledge flows and build capabilities). Practical ways to move through these stages are detailed in *KNOWledge SUCCESSion* (Shelley, 2017).

Now what opportunity number four is for knowledge professionals to play a more collaborative and proactive role in supporting the levels of knowledge maturity across organizations. This can be done through initiatives like the Knowledge Ready Organization (KRO) initiated by the Knowledge Management Society of Singapore. This initiative has evolved in to a significant value-adding developmental journey for organizations desiring to improve their performance through aligned programs of knowledge initiatives. The program mentors organizations through a balanced set of criteria in strategic cycles to sustain growth of capability and performance, as shown in Figure 10-4.

Figure 10-4. Strategic elements of the Knowledge Ready Organization

KRO is a co-created and evolving process to align the development of knowledge maturity across the six key criteria. It has been designed with the new ISO KM standard in mind and will assist organizations to achieve compliance to that standard. A self-assessment tool provides applicants with a way to assess and address the maturity level of the organization and participating in the awards provides external feedback on their progress. This is a collaborative constructive process, not a competition. The philosophy is to support the acceleration of knowledge initiatives in as many organizations as possible as higher performing organizations generate more social value for society. This approach allows mentoring of organizations through to higher levels of knowledge-driven performance over time.

This developmental approach will ensure more organizations will engage over the years and current ones can reengage to achieve the higher levels. So KRO becomes a genuine knowledge development process rather than just a competition. The multi-level and multi-dimensional benchmarks encourage beginners to engage earlier to accelerate their growth and the more experienced candidates to reengage to go to even higher levels of performance. The focus of a program about achievement of sustainable improvement, which can be appropriately given to everyone who applies. This way everyone achieves ongoing benefits based on their level of maturity and how they take next steps to improve, rather than finding "A single winner". The scoring system of ten questions for each of the six criteria ensures that those achieving higher levels of knowledge performance are recognized at a higher level, maintaining the kudos of those (and not degrading the achievements by also giving it to others who are clearly at a lower level).

KRO will be a foundation of how the knowledge profession collaborates to help the development of the profession as a whole and in doing so provide benefits of better knowledge flow to a wider society.

The fifth now what opportunity is for knowledge professionals to practice what they preach and collaborate with each other. It is ironic that internationally many other professions are more connected through professional societies than knowledge professionals are, when the fundamental principles of KM are connection, collaboration and sharing. The Knowledge Profession will benefit from creating a global identity which is recognized and respected like other societies such as CIPD (Chartered Institute for Personnel and Development) and PMI (Project Management Institute). It is difficult to have the credibility to influence government and senior decision-makers without a common identity. There is huge potential for a collective movement which fosters the cause of greater awareness of the importance of knowledge and better application of knowledge on local, national and international levels. The foundations of such a society are now being discussed by some key players in the knowledge profession with the plan to officially establish such an institution.

Attention to these five now what priorities will advance the value created by knowledge professionals and ensure that better decisions are made globally, for the benefit of "the greater good", as well as for us; the members of the profession (practitioners and academics across an eclectic mix of roles and industries). It is an exciting time for our profession to come together to create synergies to enable something greater than any one of us can be individually.

With these actions the future of the knowledge profession looks strong as we collectively become a stronger voice and build a sense of belonging for our membership. *At present there is a strong need for better use of knowledge, but not a strong enough demand from those in power.*

ABOUT THE AUTHOR

Dr Arthur Shelley is founder of Intelligent Answers, a specialist knowledge and learning advisory to industry, corporate entities, government and universities. Arthur's practice as a capability development and knowledge strategy consultant is founded on over 30 years professional experience in a variety of professional roles managing international projects in Australia, Europe, Asia and USA. As an independent educator, he has designed and facilitated Masters courses on Knowledge Management, Executive Consulting, Leadership, Applied Research Practice and Entrepreneurship in face to face and blended and on-line modes at different universities. He is a Senior Industry Fellow at RMIT University in Melbourne Australia, the author of three books, has contributed chapters for edited books, articles for academic and professional journals. In 2014 he was awarded with an Australian Office of Learning and Teaching citation for "Outstanding contributions to student learning outcomes."

Arthur is the creator and producer of international cross disciplinary interactive events such as Creative Melbourne and KMELB and is regularly invited as a speaker and workshop facilitator at international conferences. He is founder of The Organizational Zoo Ambassadors Network (an international professional peer mentoring group), creator of the RMIT University MBA mentoring program, supervisor of PhD students in 4 countries, a peer reviewer for several academic journals, co-leader of the Melbourne KM Leadership Forum and the assessor for the Knowledge Ready Organization Awards.

Before creating Intelligent Answers consultancy, he was the Global Knowledge Director for Cadbury Schweppes. As the principal of IA, he has worked with a wide range of organizations including NASA, World Bank, Singapore government, executive education services, educational institutions and research centers in several countries, HR and training organizations, government departments, fire and emergency authorities, health related, social media and creative enterprises, insurance companies, commercial banks, food manufacturers, construction and engineering firms and not-for-profits.

Full biography: https://www.linkedin.com/in/arthurshelley/
Online browsing of KNOWledge SUCCESSion:
http://www.businessexpertpress.com/books/knowledge-succession-sustained-capability-growth-through-strategic-projects.

BIBLIOGRAPHY

Bennet, A., Bennet, D., Shelley, A., Bullard, t., and Lewis, J. (2016). *The Profundity and Bifurcation of Change. The Intelligent Social Change Journey.* Frost: MQI Press.

Bloom, B. (1956-64). *Taxonomy of Educational Objectives.* New York: David McKay Company Inc.

Brown, T. (2008). Design Thinking. *Harvard Business Review,* June pp. 85-92.

Dorst, K. (2011). *The core of design thinking and its application.* New York: Elsevier.

Dweck, C. (2012). *Mindset. How you can fulfill your potential.* London: Robinson.

Frank, M., Roehrig, P. and Pring, B. (2017). *What to do when the machines do everything. How to get ahead in a world of AI, algorithms and big data.* Hoboken: John Wiley & Sons.

Johansson-Skoldberg U., Woodilla J., and Cetinkaya, M. (2013). *Design thinking: past, present and future possibilities.* New York: John Wiley & Sons.

Leavy, B. (2012). Collaborative innovation as the new imperative – design thinking, value co-creation and the power of "pull." *Strategy and Leadership* 40(2) pp. 25-34.

Liedtka, J. (2014). Innovative ways companies are using design thinking. *Strategy and Leadership* 42(2) pp. 40-45.

Maister, D., Green, C., and Galford, R. (2001). *The Trusted Advisor.* New York: The Free Press.

O'Toole G. (2016). *Quote Investigator Exploring the origins of quotations.* https://quoteinvestigator.com/2012/09/27/invent-the-future/ Accessed November 24, 2017.

Shelley, A. (2007). *The Organizational Zoo, A Survival Guide to Workplace Behavior.* Fairfield: Aslan Publishing.

Shelley, A. (2009). *Being a Successful Knowledge Leader. What knowledge practitioners need to know to make a difference.* London: ARK Publishing.

Shelley, A. (2011). Creative metaphor as a tool for stakeholder influence. Chapter 9 in: Bourne, L. *Advising Upwards, Helping management to help you.* pp 271-296. Gower Publishing.

Shelley, A. (2014). Active Learning Innovations in Knowledge Management Education Generate Higher Quality Learning Outcomes. *Journal of Entrepreneurship Management and Innovation,* Volume 10 (1) 129-145.

Shelley, A. (2015). Project Management and Leadership Education Facilitated as Projects. *International Journal of Managing Projects in Business,* Volume 8 (3) 478-490.

Shelley, A. (2017). *KNOWledge SUCCESSion Sustained capability growth through strategic projects.* Business Expert Press, USA.

Snowden, D. and Boone, M. (2007). A leaders framework for decision making. *Harvard Business Review,* October 68-76.

Weiner, E. (2016). *The Geography of Genius. The Geography of Genius. A search for the world's most creative places from ancient Athens to Silicon Valley,* New York: NY, Simon and Shuster.

Made in the USA
Columbia, SC
05 March 2018